Visitor's (

SPAIN: COSTA BRAVA :

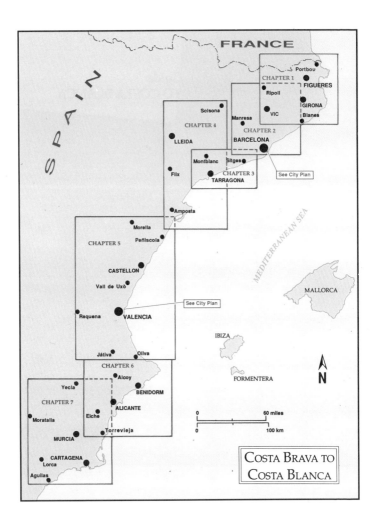

FRANCE

SPAIN

See City Plan

See City Plan

MEDITERRANEAN SEA

Portbou

CHAPTER 1

FIGUERES

Ripoll

GIRONA

VIC

Blanes

Solsona

Manresa

CHAPTER 4

CHAPTER 2

LLEIDA

BARCELONA

Montblanc

Sitges

Flix

CHAPTER 3

TARRAGONA

Amposta

Morella

Peñiscola

CHAPTER 5

CASTELLON

Vall de Uxó

MALLORCA

Requena

VALENCIA

IBIZA

Játiva

Oliva

CHAPTER 6

Alcoy

FORMENTERA

Yecla

BENIDORM

CHAPTER 7

ALICANTE

Moratalla

Elche

Torrevieja

MURCIA

CARTAGENA

Lorca

Aguilas

N

0   60 miles

0   100 km

COSTA BRAVA TO
COSTA BLANCA

VISITOR'S GUIDE
SPAIN: COSTA BRAVA to COSTA BLANCA

BARBARA MANDELL

MPC

HUNTER
PUBLISHING INC

Published by:
Moorland Publishing Co Ltd,
Moor Farm Road West,
Airfield Estate,
Ashbourne,
Derbyshire
DE6 1HD
England

© Barbara Mandell 1991

All rights reserved. No part of this
publication may be reproduced,
stored in a retrieval system, or
transmitted in any form or by any
means, electronic, mechanical,
photocopying, recording or
otherwise without the prior
permission of Moorland Publishing
Co Ltd.

British Library Cataloguing in
Publication Data:
Mandell, Barbara
    Visitor's guide to Spain:
    Costa Brava to Costa Blanca.
    - (Visitor's guides)
    I. Title II. Series
    914.604

ISBN 0 86190 426 5

Colour origination by:
Scantrans, Singapore

Printed in the UK by:
Richard Clay Ltd, Bungay, Suffolk

Cover photograph:
(International Photobank).

Illustrations have been supplied as
follows: M. Gray: pp 23 (both), 42,
63 (top), 71, 115 (top), 118 (both),
131 (bottom), 158 (bottom); Spanish
Tourist Office, London: pp 11, 27
(both), 31, 34, 38, 39, 51, 55, 59
(both), 63 (bottom), 83, 86 (both), 87
(both), 91, 94, 102, 103, 111 (both),
115 (bottom), 123 (both), 131 (top),
135 (top), 139 (top), 155 (both), 158
(top), 166 (both); J.D. Whitby: pp
14, 15, 135 (bottom), 139 (bottom),
142 (both), 143 (both).

MPC Production Team
Editor: Andrew Siddle
Designer: Jonathan Moss
Cartographer: Alastair Morrison

Published in the USA by:
Hunter Publishing Inc,
300 Raritan Center Parkway,
CN 94, Edison, NJ 08818
ISBN 1 55650 470 5 (USA)

While every care has been taken to ensure that the information in this
book is as accurate as possible at the time of publication, the publisher
and author accept no responsibility for any loss, injury or inconven-
ience sustained by anyone using this book.

CONTENTS

Key to Symbols Used in Text Margin and on Maps

♣ Parkland

Π Archaeological site

🦌 Zoo/Animal park

⚑ Golf course

✤ Garden

🎾 Sports facilities

🕳 Cave

⛪ Church/Ecclesiastical site

🏛 Building of interest

🏰 Castle/Fortification

🖼 Museum/Art gallery

🏞 Beautiful view/Scenery, Natural phenomenon

✳ Other place of interest

⛵ Watersports

Key to Maps

——— Main road

═══ Motorway

〰 River

● ▨ Town/City

✈ Airport

⬭ Lake

------ Provincial Boundary

— ·— ·— · National Boundary

How To Use This Guide

This MPC Visitor's Guide has been designed to be as easy to use as possible. Each chapter covers a region or itinerary in a natural progression which gives all the background information to help you enjoy your visit. MPC's distinctive margin symbols, the important places printed in bold, and a comprehensive index enable the reader to find the most interesting places to visit with ease. At the end of each chapter an Additional Information section gives specific details such as addresses and opening times, making this guide a complete sightseeing companion. At the back of the guide the Fact File, arranged in alphabetical order, gives practical information and useful tips to help you plan your holiday — before you go and while you are there. The maps of each region show the main towns, villages, roads and places of interest, but are not designed as route maps and motorists should always use a good recommended road atlas.

INTRODUCTION

The east coast of Spain with its three distinct regions — Catalunya (Cataluña in Castilian and Catalonia in English), the Levant and Murcia — runs down from the French frontier to the borders of Andalucía, backed by Aragón, Castilla-La Mancha and Albacete. This entire stretch of the Mediterranean seaboard has been divided up into costas, each of which has been given a name that, in some cases, describes its most outstanding characteristics.

In the far north is the Costa Brava, (the Rugged Coast) where the foothills of the Pyrénées drop down to meet the sea in a series of high cliffs honeycombed with caves and grottoes and punctured at frequent intervals by little sandy bays and isolated coves, many of them inaccessible except by boat. The only exception to this general rule is the Empordà marshland, created by a series of small rivers that run into the Golfo de Roses.

The Costa Brava ends abruptly at the port of Blanes where it meets the Costa del Maresme, distinguished by long, wide vistas of golden sand against a backdrop of distant hills that follow the shoreline down to Barcelona. Beyond the city the Costa Daurada, or Golden Coast, carries on in a similar vein past Tarragona until it merges into the Golfo de Sant Jordi and the Delta de l'Ebre. This is a vast conglomeration of sand, silt, marshes, rice paddies and wildlife. It is as flat as a board with the river threaded through to the furthest point, largely surrounded by the Mediterranean.

On the opposite side of this promontory, much of which is taken up by the Parc Natural del Delta de l'Ebre, is the Costa del Azahar. This is known as the Orange Blossom Coast due to the citrus orchards blanketing the fertile plains of Castellón and Valencia and spilling over the main highways almost down to the water's edge. The beaches here are sandy but with fewer large coastal resorts.

Hills, rather than mountains, start to reappear on the Costa Blanca, famous for its unusually clear skies which led the Greeks to call their early settlement *Akra Leuka* (the White Citadel), and the Romans to rename it the City of Light. One of the most impressive of its many rocky outcrops is the Peñon de Ifach, near Calpe, which looks remarkably like a miniature Gibraltar. The shoreline lacks the grandeur of the Costa Brava but makes up for it with some beautiful sandy beaches, especially on either side of Alicante. Finally, the Costa Cálida fully justifies its reputation as the Warm Coast, offering a variety of attractions including an enormous lagoon called the Mar Menor. This is separated from the sea by a giant sandspit known as La Manga, with highrise apartment blocks, hotels and other holiday facilities.

The scenery is not the only thing that changes from one costa to another. Catalunya, consisting of the provinces of Girona, Barcelona, Tarragona and Lleida, prefers to use Catalan rather than Castilian Spanish, although both are its official languages. As a result, the region is known as Cataluña elsewhere, Costa Dorada is more widely used in other parts of the country than Costa Daurada, Roses may well become Rosas, Lleida turns into Lérida and even *plaça* is transformed into *plaza* beyond the regional borders with Aragón and the Levant. The latter comprises Castellón and Valencia on the Costa del Azahar as well as Alicante's Costa Blanca whereas Murcia corresponds to the Costa Cálida and is an entity all on its own.

Despite their occasional language differences and variations in local government, the six costas have many things in common. These include mountains rising up to the Meseta, a huge plateau that covers much of central Spain; rivers like the Ebre, the Jucar and the Segura; natural lagoons and man-made reservoirs; game parks and wildlife reserves. The most memorable of these are the Parc Natural dels Aiguamolls de l'Empordà, the Parc Natural del Delta de l'Ebre and the Parc Natural de la Zona Volcànica de la Garrotxa in the foothills of the Pyrénées. There are extensive areas devoted to maize and cereals, terraced vineyards overlooking fertile valleys, rice paddies, almond trees, olive groves and citrus orchards. Industry is centred mainly on Barcelona, Tarragona, Valencia and, to a lesser extent, Cartagena, while fishing fleets operate from selected ports.

The population is very unevenly distributed. Catalunya is one of the most densely populated areas in Spain, mainly because of its rapid industrial development, centred around Barcelona. Villages and hamlets become progressively more widely spaced and isolated the further one travels inland until there are some districts with hardly any inhabitants and only an occasional town of any size. Nevertheless, there is plenty of evidence to show that people have been occupying the whole peninsula since prehistoric times. Caves, some of them decorated with modest rock paintings, as well as dolmens and traces of early settlements, have been discovered in many places. They are of great interest although they do not compare with the caves of Altamira or the burial chambers of Antequera in Andalucía.

The Iberians established their own communities in places like Ullastret and at intervals along the coast, while the Greeks set up trading posts, only to have them taken over by the Romans and the Visigoths. Both of these sets of intruders created new towns or adapted existing centres to suit their own requirements, leaving behind some substantial ruins. The Moors were skilful at building fortifications on strategic hilltops throughout the area, to such an extent that it is difficult to follow any scenic route without passing the remains of an ancient fortress that has either been restored or is earmarked for attention in the near future. The Arabs also introduced efficient irrigation systems and methods of farming that have remained almost unchanged for more than 1,000 years.

After the Reconquest the Christians replaced mosques with churches and cathedrals, strengthened and extended existing defences, founded monasteries and added palaces as well as town and country residences. Art flourished, along with literature and music, but suffered during the War of Succession and the periodical uprisings culminating in the bitter Civil War of the 1930s.

Modernists, one of the most famous being the architect Antoni Gaudí, introduced a host of new ideas, methods and colours at the turn of the century. They incorporated the best of Roman and Moorish art, created new and often fantastic shapes of their own and built or adapted churches, private houses and even apartment blocks within a wide radius of Barcelona. Painting took on a new dimension in the hands of Picasso and Salvador Dali, Pau Casals was acknowledged as one of the world's greatest cellists while Andrés Segovia raised the guitar to the status of a classical instrument.

Judging from the various cave paintings, it would seem that in prehistoric times the country was constantly being invaded, either from Morocco and Algeria or by tribes from other parts of Europe who made occasional sorties across the Pyrénées. Mostly they seem to have settled about 3 days' journey on foot from the coast at places like Cogul in Lleida, Valltorta near Castellón and Cantos de la Visera in Murcia. The Bronze Age inhabitants left behind fragments of pottery while the later Iberian sculptures show the men on horseback, armed with swords, spears and daggers, and the women dressed in hooded cloaks with long swallow-tail sleeves and attractive jewellery.

The Iberians built themselves a succession of walled towns at strategic points such as Tarragona and Cartagena but these were captured and destroyed by the Carthaginians who did little to replace them with anything designed to last. The Greeks, on the other hand, who founded Marseilles in 600BC, established new colonies at places like Denia and Empúries where a whole fortified town has been excavated a stone's throw from the beach.

When Carthage finally lost out to Rome in 201BC the Spanish costas found themselves in very different hands, obliged to do as they were told but rewarded with a period of peace and prosperity that continued almost uninterrupted for about 500 years. However, when the Roman Empire foundered, and the Visigoths moved in, Spain was soon back in a state of flux, unstable with no hope of any improvement for the next two centuries or more.

Eventually help arrived in the guise of the Moors, fresh from their successful invasion of Andalucía in AD711 and determined to press on northwards across the Pyrénées. Most people, apart from the Visigoths, were delighted to welcome them; Jews were released from persecution, and Christians were allowed to worship as they chose, provided they made no trouble and paid their taxes regularly. Even serfs were given a certain measure of freedom.

Although Arab rule was comparatively tolerant, the Christians refused to give in and in AD801 the Franks recaptured Barcelona under Charlemagne. They occupied the surrounding area and installed a number of Visigoth nobles to administer it for them until, less than 100 years later, the region achieved its independence. In 1137 the Count of Barcelona married the heiress to the throne of Aragon, thereby uniting the two ruling houses. However, the citizens were determined to keep their options open and the Aragonese oath of allegiance made this perfectly clear. It stated 'We, who are as good as you, swear to you, who are no better than we, to accept you as our king and sovereign lord, provided you observe all our liberties and laws, but, if not, not.' The agreement seemed to work perfectly and soon Barcelona acquired an empire that included several Mediterranean islands, parts of Greece and a stretch of coastline from Valencia to Roussillon.

Constant friction between Aragón and neighbouring Castile was

Watersports are very popular on the eastern costas

finally ended by the marriage of Ferdinand and Isabel, both of whom succeeded to their respective thrones. However, instead of reaping any substantial benefits from the alliance, Catalunya soon discovered that it was expected to hand over a large percentage of the funds needed for the reconquest of the rest of Spain. Isabel, energetic and devout, and Ferdinand, who was subtle and unscrupulous, complemented each other perfectly. Together they recaptured Granada in 1492, curbed the powers of the nobility and earned the title of Catholic monarchs, bestowed by Pope Innocent VIII. They also created the Inquisition with the help of Pope Sixtus IV.

The Inquisition rapidly grew from the authorised nucleus of three or four virtuous and learned men into a nationwide organisation, totally disinterested in the political divisions between Castile, Aragon, Valencia and Catalunya but dedicated to furthering the interests of the crown. The Jews were hounded out of their traditional quarters in places like Girona, the remaining Muslims were forced to become Christians or seek asylum elsewhere, and even the discovery of America and the treasures that flowed in from the New World were of little benefit to the eastern regions of the country.

Conditions did not improve very much under their grandson, Charles V, nor under his successors, who were constantly demanding additional men and money to finance and carry out their various overseas expeditions. Sometimes these were successful, as in the defeat of the Turks at Lepanto, while other ventures failed miserably with far reaching consequences, the most spectacular being the loss of the Armada which sailed against England in 1588. The result was national bankruptcy. Philip IV was applauded for his early victories during the Thirty Years War. However, when it came to paying for them, Valencia raised all kinds of objections, only changing its tune when the king walked out of the Cortes in Lleida, threatening to authorise reprisals.

Meanwhile Richelieu, who had advised Philip to be content with his position as King of Portugal, Aragon and Valencia and Count of Barcelona, took matters into his own hands and sent French troops into Spanish Roussillon. The Thirty Years War ended but fighting between the two countries dragged on. The prolonged conflict, combined with corruption in high places, revolts and uprisings, crippling taxes and poor crops, all helped to bring Spain to its knees.

When Charles II died in 1700 without an heir, he left his impoverished and exhausted country to Philip of Anjou, the grandson of his cousin Louis XIV. However, another member of the family, the Archduke Charles of Austria, had been promised the throne under a treaty signed by France, England and the United Provinces and was determined to fight for his rights. Everyone with a vested interest joined in the resulting War of Spanish Succession which ended with the Treaty of Utrecht in 1713. This gave Gibraltar to Britain and the rest of Spain to Philip, provided the country was never united with France. Barcelona, Valencia and Aragon had sided with Charles and suffered accordingly.

The kings who succeeded Philip varied a great deal. The best of them were Ferdinand VI, who believed in peace, scholarship and curbing the powers of the Inquisition, and Charles III, a benevolent despot under whose guidance the country began to prosper. His foreign policy was dictated by an intense dislike of England which was not improved by two unsuccessful attempts to retake Gibraltar by force. However, he had his revenge by supporting the revolutionary movement during the American War of Independence, with the result that Florida was returned to the Spanish fold.

Unfortunately, Charles IV inherited none of his father's admirable qualities. He was stupid and lazy and very much under the thumb of his domineering wife. The family compact with Louis XVI ended when the French king went to the guillotine, with the result that the newly created Republic sent in an invasion force that burned and looted its way down through Catalunya to the border with Valencia. The ensuing treaty tied Spain to France's apron strings and involved a combined attack on England that ended at the Battle of Cape St Vincent when the Spanish fleet was forced back into Cádiz.

Napoleon's return from Egypt made matters even worse. The remainder of the fleet was lost at Trafalgar and Prince Ferdinand was arrested for plotting against his father. This gave Napoleon an excuse to send in more troops, lure the king and his family to Bayonne and install his brother Joseph as King of Spain. It all looked too easy until the Spaniards rose in revolt. Britain went to the assistance of Portugal, and the Duke of Wellington's campaign, combined with the disastrous retreat from Moscow, forced Napoleon to withdraw from the Peninsular War.

Released by France and safely on the throne, Ferdinand VII proved to be as bad, if not worse, than any of his predecessors. There were revolts at home and in the American colonies, most of which achieved their independence, followed by the First Carlist War after his death in 1833. This was a battle for the crown between the supporters of his infant daughter Isabel and those of his brother Don Carlos who was eventually forced to admit defeat. Things were no better under Isabel II but the royalists persisted and, after the revolution of 1868, the crown was offered to a series of likely candidates. They included Prince Amedeo of Savoy who accepted the nomination but resigned at the first convenient opportunity.

The First Republic was proclaimed in 1870 but, after a few turbulent years, Alfonso XII, then 17 years old and at school in England, was called back to restore the Bourbon dynasty. Alfonso XIII, born 6 months after his father's death in 1885, inherited a country that was deeply divided and in a state of ferment which reached its climax in 1931. He failed to abdicate but agreed to leave Spain, sailing from Cartagena for France, upon which the revolutionary committee became the provisional government of the Second Republic. This lasted longer than the first but had no greater chance of success.

Spain was in the melting pot again; seething with discontent, torn by political rivalries and heading inexorably for civil war. When the army in Spanish Morocco mutinied, the revolt spread to the mainland within 2 days but uprisings in Madrid and Barcelona were put down and the Republicans were confident of success. However, a mercenary force of well-trained Moors from North Africa, led by Francisco Franco, captured most of Andalucía. Germany, Italy and

The plant life of this region is rich and varied

Portugal sent troops and planes to help the Nationalists, while Russia provided supplies for the Republicans and organised the famous International Brigade. Observers like Ernest Hemingway, George Orwell and Willy Brandt kept a watching brief while Britain and France set up a non-intervention committee.

The Civil War, with hideous atrocities on both sides, lasted for nearly 3 years and cost about 1 million lives. Franco assumed control, punished the regions that had opposed him, set about repairing part of the damage and maintained a somewhat doubtful, one-sided neutrality during World War II. In 1953 Franco signed a treaty with the United States, exchanging naval and air bases for much needed dollars, and conditions began to improve considerably, although he had no intention of changing his basic ideas. However, his long-term plans were dashed when Admiral Carrero Blanco was killed by terrorists in 1973. With no-one else to succeed him, Franco decided to restore the monarchy, nominating Juan Carlos who had the advantage of being Alfonso XIII's grandson and seemed to be quite manageable.

At first Don Carlos, who had succeeded the dictator in 1975, did nothing to rock the boat but, little by little, he steered his country back towards democracy with the help of men like Adolfo Suarez. Press

The heat of the day occasionally calls for some cooling off

censorship was abolished, elections were held for the first time for more than 30 years and an attempted coup fizzled out on the orders of the king. After the Socialists swept to power in 1982, Spain found herself with a popular king and a popular prime minister in Felipe Gonzalez, membership of both NATO and the EEC and brighter prospects for the future than at any time for at least 500 years.

Food and Drink

Places to eat in the region include everything from expensive, elegant international restaurants to small wayside inns providing simple, traditional food. Between these extremes there are hotel diningrooms, run-of-the-mill restaurants with standard menus, atmospheric little places offering both familiar dishes and local specialities, seafood restaurants where everything is fresh and usually delicious and reasonably cheap cafeterias and cafés. There are also some foreign restaurants, usually Chinese or Italian, as well as pizza parlours, American fast food houses and little shacks along the beach, often serving excellent roast sardines.

Despite this abundance of choice, some of the most fascinating places for a snack are the innumerable *tapas* bars where a whole selection of local delicacies are served with the drinks. *Tapas* literally means 'lids', tiny saucers that hold just enough to whet the appetite but not sufficient to make you feel uncomfortable about leaving something you do not like. Dishes of everything from shellfish, squid or little pieces of meat to garlic mushrooms, vegetables, egg, olives and nuts are displayed in glass cases on the counter. The best method is to order a *porción*, or small helping, of one or two that appeal to you and go back for a *ración*, or larger plate, of anything that comes up to expectations. Spaniards often visit these bars at around 7.30 or 8pm and order enough to tide them over until dinner, generally about 2 or 3 hours later.

Both the *menú del día* (menu of the day) and the à la carte items are posted up outside the restaurants, making it possible to see exactly what is on offer and the various prices before sitting down to eat. The set menus generally turn out to be cheaper than ordering a similar number of individual courses. Bread and water are usually provided but drinks and coffee are extra. It is better to choose a fairly crowded restaurant rather than one with an attractive decor but very few customers, because the Spaniards enjoy their food and know where to go for good quality at realistic prices. They tend to linger over a large lunch at about 1.30 or 2pm and seldom think of dinner before 10pm or even later. However, with the growth of tourism, some restaurants in the leading resorts may open at about 8.30pm to accommodate their foreign visitors. A service charge may or may not be added to the bill so it is necessary to make sure and tip accordingly.

SPECIALITIES

One of the many delights of a holiday in Spain is the opportunity to try out a variety of traditional dishes quite unlike anything you would find at home. Most of the ingredients will be very similar but the blending of flavours and the methods of preparation are so individual that the specialities of one area can taste subtly different from those of the region next door.

With so many fishing fleets based along the eastern costas of Spain it is hardly surprising that seafood of all descriptions has pride of place on the list. The Costa Brava is known for its thick angler soup and for lobsters prepared with roasted almonds and garlic. Tarragona favours *arroz abanda* which consists of as many different types of fish as possible, all cooked together and served with rice, whereas Valencia practically invented paella. Although this is served almost everywhere, the recipes vary enormously, not only between different provinces but also from one restaurant to another. The Costa del Azahar insists that it offers the original and therefore the best, which must be cooked over a wood fire and contain ingredients like snails and young beans. However, opinions differ, even to the extent that it can be made from either fish or meat, or a combination of the two, combined with rice. Alternatively, *fiduea* consists of fish and shellfish prepared with thin noodles instead of rice. The Costa Cálida still uses ideas introduced by the Moors which give its dishes a distinctive flavour. Among many that are worth trying are *el arroz al caldero, caldero al estilo del Mar Menor*, which is a kind of fish stew, and *mujol* roe which is delicious.

Meat stews of all descriptions are the staple diet in most of the inland areas and may contain anything from rabbit or pig's trotters to chicken, lamb or kid with a variety of mountain herbs and vegetables. Turkeys, geese and ducks are flavoured with unusual stuffings, while roast lamb or kid may be served with a sauce introduced by the Romans. Ham, meat pies and all types of sausages appear regularly on the menus.

Vegetables can be a feature in their own right, especially on the Costa Cálida where the heart of a lettuce is divided into sections and dressed with a special sauce. Young artichokes are fried on their own or with tomatoes; beans and asparagus may be served alone or with scrambled eggs, while beaten egg is used for the crust of *arroz con costra*, a tasty concoction baked in the oven, that originated in Elche.

On the whole, sweets and cheeses come as something of an anticlimax, consisting mainly of fruit tarts, crème caramel and assorted ices. However, one or two prove to be a little unusual, among them *la collá*, a type of yoghurt made in Castellón with the pistils of wild artichokes, and *turron* which, like some of the other sweetmeats, is a legacy from the Moors.

A variety of wines are produced along the eastern costas although most of them are virtually unknown outside their own regions. The heavier reds come, for the most part, from Catalunya and the majority of whites from Valencia. Murcia has some excellent vineyards in the Jumilla area whose light reds and rosés are claimed to be among the best in Spain. Valencia also produces a refreshing summer drink called *horchata*. *Sangria* is wine, reinforced with spirits and liqueurs according to each barman's favourite recipe, and served in a jug with a veritable fruit salad floating on the top. Teetotallers will find all the fresh orange juice they can possibly drink.

Religious and Secular Festivals

Spain is justly famous for its many colourful fairs and festivals, some of which are religious while others commemorate historical events or have their origins in ancient pagan rites. Among the most impressive are the Holy Week festivities when statues of Christ and the Virgin Mary, as well as complete tableaux, are paraded through the streets on splendidly decorated platforms that may need forty or more young men to carry them. Corpus Christi and the Assumption of the Virgin are equally solemn occasions, marked by processions and the appearance of members of the Brotherhoods in their monk-like habits and tall, conical hoods with slits for the eyes, recalling the worst excesses of the Inquisition.

In addition to these nationwide events, nearly every town and village has its own patron saint who is honoured in a similar but less elaborate fashion. Then there are semi-religious occasions such as the appearance of the Three Kings at Epiphany loaded with sweets and toys for the children, and annual processions to isolated sanctuaries that usually start out as pilgrimages and end up as gigantic picnics. Carnival, which was prohibited by the Inquisition and later by Franco, is being revived all over the country with the help of grotesque masks, fancy dress costumes, feasting, traditional music, satirical songs and dancing. It probably dates from the time of the Romans but now marks the beginning of Lent and provides an excellent excuse for letting off steam before embarking on 40 days of abstinence. The traditional songs and dances are carefully preserved, along with all the colourful costumes that vary from one region to another.

The Nights of Fire, the most famous of which is the Fallas in Valencia, give everyone an opportunity to get rid of all the clutter that has accumulated during the past 12 months and at the same time welcome back the spring. These are followed in due course by spring fairs, summer fiestas and harvest festivals, after which it is time to take a short break before starting all over again.

The ancient battles between the Moors and the Christians are re-enacted in early December with sumptuous costumes, spirited horses, enormous enthusiasm and large quantities of gunpowder. Between times there are bullfights, football matches and other sporting events, as well as concerts, folk festivals and local galas, many with highly individual touches such as acrobatic feats or unique dishes.

1

COSTA BRAVA

Until comparatively recently, the Costa Brava was the best known area for popular holiday resorts in Spain. The name was used, albeit inaccurately, to include the shoreline south of Barcelona and made much of Sitges on its somewhat localised Costa de Garraf. Sitges itself was a seething mass of sun-toasted humanity before the Costa Blanca and the Costa del Sol rose up in a welter of concrete and plate glass to capture their share of tourists for centres like Benidorm and Torremolinos. Then, as now, it was within easy reach of holiday-makers from the far side of the Pyrénées. The main attractions included beautiful sandy beaches, impressive scenery, historic sites and established resorts like Lloret de Mar, in addition to brilliant sunshine, pine forests and delicious traditional seafood.

More recently, the area has joined enthusiastically in the nation-wide competition for package tours and a place in the glossy inter-national travel brochures. Fortunately the Costa Brava has also managed to preserve a great deal of its original charm, thereby appealing to individual visitors who prefer a measure of solitude to lively all-night discos.

Costa Brava was the name given at the turn of the century to the Girona shoreline between Portbou, facing Cerbère across the fron-tier, and the fishing port of Blanes, some 60km (40 miles) north-east of Barcelona. The former is a fairly typical border town tucked away at the end of an inlet with an international railway station, a small dock and one or two rather basic hotels. There is no particular reason for stopping there and **Llançà**, slightly further down the coast, is more convenient for anyone who is determined to inspect the isolated and largely ruined Benedictine monastery of Sant Quirze de Colera. It was built in the eleventh century on the site of an earlier church and still has the remains of its cloister, a few attendant buildings and fragments of the original fortifications. For energetic sightseers the best way of getting there is along the GR11 through Vilamaniscle. However, there is also a steep mountain track leading up from the village for motorists who are prepared to negotiate it slowly and carefully.

Llançà is a small but popular seaside resort that is making long-term plans for the future which include the construction of a new dock area with berths for 450 pleasure craft and a special basin for the trawler fleet. Most of the fishing fraternity live by the sea whereas the rest of the community seem to prefer the hillside behind. There are some fairly modest but quite acceptable hotels, a variety of restaurants, a pleasantly flat beach and the small church of Sant Vicenç. An added bonus is that a good secondary road connects Llançà with Figueres, the most important town in the vicinity.

Figueres, roughly 36km (23 miles) from the border, is the first place of any size on the main route to the south with the motorway bypassing it on one side and the N11 forming a neat loop round the other. It is a very agreeable, smallish town with a good selection of hotels, including the Hotel Ampurdán which is on the outskirts of the town and has three stars (☎ 972 50 05 62). There are also some excellent restaurants. Figueres gets overcrowded during the summer, so anyone who plans to stop there for the night would be wise to book in advance (see the Additional Information section at the end of the chapter for the Tourist Office's address and telephone number). Despite its eighteenth-century castle and toy museum, it might never have attracted a great deal of attention if Salvador Dali had not been born there in 1904. Although much of his life was spent elsewhere — in Paris, the United States and Portlligat on the Golf de Roses — Figueres held a special place in his affections. In 1961 Dali decided that the burned out shell of the municipal theatre, one of the many casualties of the Civil War, was exactly what he wanted for his proposed museum. Once the complicated negotiations were completed he set to work designing every detail of what he extravagantly predicted would be the spiritual centre of Europe. It opened with a grand flourish in September 1974 and is now said to have more visitors than any other museum in Spain apart from the famous Prado in Madrid.

The exterior, partly icing-sugar pink and partly elegant in the style of the nineteenth century, is enlivened by statues, including a deep sea diver lounging against the parapet, which give an indication of things to come. For example, when seen from a distance, a nude painting of Dali's wife Gala looking through a window at the Mediterranean turns out to be a portrait of Abraham Lincoln. The painted ceiling of the Salón Noble is dominated by the artist's two enormous bare feet as he reaches up to offer a tribute to the swirling clouds of the savage north wind known as the Tramontana. Then there is the Mae West Room, viewed through elaborately draped curtains with a plump scarlet settee in front of a double fireplace flanked by two Parisian scenes. It is not particularly memorable until a special lens transforms it into a portrait of the lady in question with pouting lips, a flattish nose, half-closed eyes and a cascade of golden curls.

As well as his own works, Dali included a number of other items that appealed to him — a costume made from giant sequins by Paco Rabanne who was once an extrovert part of the Paris fashion scene, and an example of the type of furniture designed by the architect Antoni Gaudí. A voluptuous, Medusa-like figure is perched on the bonnet of a car while the original stage has an enormous backdrop of a torso bowing its head in the direction of a surprisingly lifelike orchestra. Another very personalised aspect of the Teatro-Museo Dali is that there is no entrance fee on 6 January, the Day of the Three Kings, traditionally associated with presents and therefore an appropriate time for Dali's annual gift to his home town.

Not all the exhibits in the museum are surrealist. One very popular example of his early work is the *Church at Cadaqués from Port Alguer at Eight O'clock in the Morning*, painted when he was 20 years old. The scene at **Cadaqués** is easily identifiable today with its collection of white houses clustered round a tiny bay on Cap de Creus, about 30km (20 miles) away. Although it has been a popular haunt of writers and artists for nearly half a century, this ancient fishing village is largely unspoiled, having made a conscious effort to preserve much of its original atmosphere. However, it has also moved with the times. On one hand there are narrow, winding streets and little boats on the sand while, on the other, buildings like the Casa Serinyena and the Escoles introduce a modernistic note along with sculptures by Josep Llimona in the old cemetery over-looking the sea. The resort has two well equipped hotels and at least one first class restaurant but the beaches, although most attractive, are on the small side and parking spaces are almost non-existent. Cadaqués' other attractions include its Museum of Art and the Perrot-Moore Museum of European Graphic Art. The church, with its surprisingly ornate Baroque altarpiece, plays host to the International Music Festival held every summer.

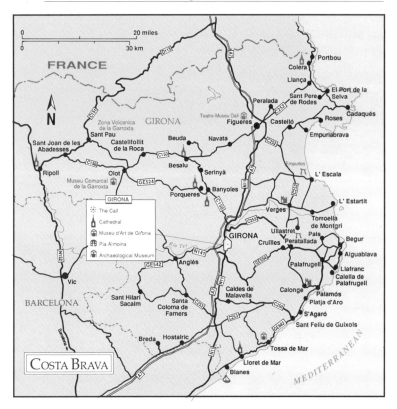

The scenery around Cadaqués is some of the most spectacular on the Costa Brava. Little roads clamber up and down this outpost of the Pyrénées, one of them skirting the fine natural harbour on its way to Cap de Creus, the most easterly point on the Iberian Peninsula. The cliffs are deeply serrated with isolated bays and minute coves, some of them inaccessible except by boat and then only with extreme caution because of the constant danger from tiny islands, jagged rocks and unexpected shoals. The area is exceptionally popular with divers and underwater fishermen, particularly around the island of Messina. Today the mountainsides are rather bare, the vegetation consisting mainly of scrub, but during the Middle Ages they were covered with dense forest, a large proportion of which came under the jurisdiction of the Benedictine monastery of Sant Pere de Rodes.

This magnificent example of feudal architecture began life about

Teatro-Museo Dali, Figueres

The atmospheric fishing village of Cadaqués

1,000 years ago on the site of a pagan temple, perched like an eagle's nest above the Golfo de Lion, with magnificent views along the coast. Legend has it that the monastery was established after a number of sacred relics, including the head of St Peter, were sent over from Rome for safekeeping and hidden in a cave in the vicinity. When the danger had passed and the time came to return them, the cave and everything in it had miraculously disappeared. Building work started almost at once, ostensibly to mark the site but possibly also to provide an opportunity for the relic to come to light again. Whatever the truth of the matter, Sant Pere de Rodes was a force to be reckoned with until it was abandoned in the nineteenth century when, like so many other powerful religious centres, it was deprived of its lands and other possessions.

Nowadays, Sant Pere de Rodes has been declared a National Monument and strenuous efforts are being made to repair the worst of the damage. Apart from the church with its tall bell tower, ancient crypt and the remains of the cloister, there are a few rather bedraggled buildings still standing, partly enclosed in the original walls and watched over by a sturdy keep.

On the opposite side of the mountains, south-west of Cadaqués, is the beautiful Golfo de Roses whose busy fishing port is the oldest in Catalunya. It was originally the site of a Greek settlement called *Rhode*, of which very little is known at the moment although excavations are going on to try to find out something more about it.

For several centuries **Roses** was an important trading centre but the port suffered eventually because of the lack of modern dock facilities. As a result it turned its attention to fishing and building up a lucrative tourist industry. Villas and apartment blocks appeared almost overnight, prime sites were chosen for new holiday hotels, some with enough space for tennis courts and swimming pools, and a handful of campsites were established in the vicinity. All this, together with long and sandy beaches, ideal conditions for a whole range of water sports, and one or two antiquated ruins, have kept it very much in the public eye. The ruins include the remains of a sixteenth-century fortress and part of a church that was once attached to the monastery of Santa María de Roses. The large fishing fleet occupies most of the harbour, landing about 3,000 tons a year, the day's catch being auctioned off each evening at the Lonja.

Roses is well placed for visiting the many dolmens and prehistoric standing stones that have been discovered all over the area. It is also within easy reach of Figueres, Vilabertran, with its representative collection of elderly buildings, and **Peralada**, which is known for its still and sparkling wines. This historic little town has many old buildings of its own as well as a small local museum and an elegant casino housed in the much restored medieval castle with appropriate furniture and a very viewable display of pictures and tapestries. For anyone who enjoys walking, the GR92 passes by on its way from Portbou to the border with Valencia, a route which takes it through the Parc Natural dels Aiguamolls de l'Empordà.

At one time the Empordà marshes covered nearly all the Golfo de Roses and extended inland beyond Castelló, where there was a large lake, and down to the Iberian town of Ullastret. They receded gradually in the face of encroaching rice paddies and meadows that were reclaimed and used for raising cattle and, not so long ago, were in grave danger of disappearing altogether under a blanket of modern tourist facilities. However, in 1983 the Catalan parliament saved the day by creating an official nature reserve where visitors are welcome provided they obey the rules. These include keeping to the marked footpaths, avoiding 'No Entry' zones and causing as little aggravation as possible to the local people and the birds and animals. Camping is forbidden except on the designated sites, dogs must be kept on leads and no plants or any of the wild creatures, whether alive or dead, may be removed from the reserve.

Vegetation in the park ranges from trees like poplars, ash, elm and willows to reeds and grasses, purple and yellow iris and buttercups. Small animals such as voles and shrews share this natural habitat with weasels, polecats, badgers and red foxes as well as a few wild boar, although these are usually found in the Serra de Verdera mountains. Nearly 300 different types of birds have been seen at one time or another; they include purple herons, white storks, golden plovers, bee-eaters, kingfishers, owls, buzzards and kestrels, as well as an occasional flamingo. The best time for bird watching is in the morning or the early evening from any of the special lookout points. Binoculars are invaluable and so is an ample supply of insect repellent, although the bats do their best to keep down the mosquito population. It is also a good idea to take along a pair of rubber boots if it has been raining, especially near the lakes and lagoons, and to dress as unobtrusively as possible.

As can be expected with so much sea and sand about, one or two holiday centres are growing up on the coast with marinas designed especially for pleasure craft. The largest is **Empuriabrava**, slightly north of the Río La Muga's mouth. It is concentrated along two large canals and more than twenty smaller ones with 2,500 berths, some of them private moorings in the residential area, each attached to its respective holiday villa. Visitors' moorings, roughly 170 in all, are near the sailing club close to the harbour mouth which is 50m (160ft) wide, with a depth of 3m (10ft), and has no hidden rocks to worry about. There are all the usual facilities, a restaurant and a swimming pool but, so far, not much in the way of hotels or adjacent campsites.

At the opposite end of the Golfo de Roses is the small natural port of **L'Escala** whose main interest is in catching and salting anchovies, as it has been doing for many years. Despite the fact that the modern sector can provide most of the same amenities as Empuriabrava, its chief attraction is undoubtedly Empúries, an impressive conglomeration of ruins with strong Iberian, Greek and Roman connections, located nearby. The Greek colony was founded in about 600BC as a kind of extension to *Massilia*, the present day Marseilles, and within 100 years had grown into a self-governing community based on trade with the interior. The Romans, under Scipios, landed there in 218BC and almost at once began to establish their own city which was eventually superseded by *Tarraco*, now Tarragona. It grew steadily in size and importance but declined almost as rapidly and was abandoned at the end of the third century AD, leaving only a few hangers-on in Sant Marti d'Empúries which is still inhabited.

Until quite recently, it was thought that the Romans had built over the existing Greek foundations but a series of excavations have proved beyond any doubt that the two cities existed side by side. The earlier complex, dating from about the fifth century BC, is virtually on the seashore and has the remains of dozens of different buildings such as temples and taverns, an arcaded market, a public cistern, watch towers and a salting plant. The Romans installed themselves further up the hillside where they built villas, a forum and an amphitheatre as well as temples and various aids to gracious living, enclosed in their own stone walls. There is even a section of the original breakwater, said to be one of the very few early harbour installations still existing in the Mediterranean. Empúries also has an archaeological centre and a small museum on the site as well as facilities for visiting students and people involved in research. Although machines are placed strategically at various points on the site and by putting money in these you can hear information about the remains, the official guidebook is better value.

Beyond L'Escala are the cliffs of the Montgrí Massif, full of exceptionally beautiful caves and strange rock formations like El Forat, pierced by a lopsided, tunnel-like opening large enough to sail through in good weather. One kilometre ($^1/_2$ mile) or so offshore, facing L'Estartit, are the Medes, two islands surrounded by rocks of

A view of Puerto de la Selva from the monastery of Sant Pere de Rodes

Ruins at Empúries

assorted sizes. At one time they were much favoured by pirates as a base for raids along the coast. One of them, Meda Gran, has a lighthouse and the remains of a few buildings left over from the days when it was inhabited. The seabed all around the Medes has been described as an underwater paradise and is now an official marine park which divers can explore at their leisure. However, fishing is strictly forbidden and so is the removal of anything, such as pieces of rock, which could be even remotely described as souvenirs.

Inland from L'Estartit is **Torroella de Montgrí** where James II, the Count of Barcelona, built a fortress in 1294 to protect what was then a busy port. The sea receded, leaving the town surrounded by a fertile plain. However, his royal palace, known as El Mirador, was rebuilt about 100 years ago and is one of the other local attractions, along with the atmospheric Plaça Major, two small churches and the remains of its defending walls and towers. A little further along the road to the north-west is **Verges**, justly famous for its centuries-old Dance of Death. During Holy Week a number of the inhabitants, wearing very realistic skulls and tightly fitting costumes painted to represent skeletons, take part in a primitive ritual to the strains of a medieval dirge. They are accompanied by others dressed as skeletons in monks' habits, as was the custom in the fourteenth century when Europe was often stricken with the plague.

From Verges a secondary road joins the C255 between Girona and Palafrugell with plenty of interesting places to visit nearby. These include the ruined Iberian settlement at Ullastret with its well preserved walls and a small museum housed in an old hermitage at the entrance. The town itself has a selection of medieval walls and towers and an interesting Gothic trade exchange where fairs and markets were held during the Middle Ages.

A short distance away is **Peratallada**, a delightful village where most of the historic buildings date from around the thirteenth century. There are two castles, a number of old houses lining the narrow streets and three walled enclosures that were the main line of defence in the days when it belonged to the Cruïlles family. **Cruïlles** itself was dominated by the former Benedictine monastery of Sant Miguel whose abbey church still has the remains of its mural paintings. However, a splendid beam, carved with monks, was transferred some time ago to the Museu d'Art de Girona.

Located east of Peratallada, the village of **Pals** has everything going for it — attractive surroundings, an extremely fascinating medieval quarter, the ancient castle with its Romanesque clock tower and even a centuries-old water tank, in addition to some original walls and the Gothic church of Sant Pere. There is also an excellent golf course surrounded by pine woods practically on the beach with a restaurant, a sports shop and equipment such as clubs and electric trolleys for hire. It is open throughout the year, except on Tuesdays from September to June. The shoreline is equally inviting, stretching for about 9km (5 miles), interrupted briefly by the Río Ter, with the GR92 following it for much of the way. The sandy stretch ends quite abruptly at the Raco Rocks, marking the northern end of the Cap de Begur massif.

The high, white market town of **Begur**, dominated by its mouldering castle set apart on the top of a hill, makes an ideal stopping place for anyone who wants to explore the surrounding area at leisure. Apart from the local hostelries there are two comfortable and well equipped hotels, one of them a modern *parador*, at Aiguablava less than 4km (2¹/₂ miles) to the south. The Pals golf course is just as accessible 5km (3 miles) away in the opposite direction. Pals also has a restored fourteenth-century quarter which is carefully restored to house several craftshops. The countryside all round is dotted with *masos*, old farmhouses that were once obliged to fortify themselves against attacks by pirates, and nearly every village has something of interest to offer. It may be a ceramics workshop, a choral group specialising in the Havaneres (romantic songs brought back from Cuba by the local sailors), a popular *sadana* dance band, a colourful open-air market or the remains of some early fortifications.

The rugged cliffs are full of tiny inlets and spectacular caves like En Gispert which can be explored on foot by anyone who has a torch or a lantern. Others, like the colourful Cova del Bisbe, can only be reached by boat. At one time Begur earned its living from coral which was collected by divers and turned into jewellery but during the last century the inhabitants decided that cork was not only an equally profitable industry but a much less hazardous one.

Palafrugell, to the south-west, is the main town in Catalunya as far as manufacturing cork is concerned and has a large Modernist factory with a wrought iron façade and a metal tower to underline the fact. The local architecture generally tends to be Art Nouveau rather than traditional, which makes a change from ancient stone. The Casa de Cultura Josep Pla, named after its popular writer, houses a small municipal museum. This vies for attention with a busy Sunday market, the nearby hermitage of Sant Sebastià de la Guarda, the castle and gardens of Cap Roig and the popular holiday playgrounds of Llafranc and Calella de Palafrugell. These are linked by a road that wanders round the bay. Calella is an attractive fishing village and a good place to listen to the Havaneres in early summer, sung from a boat anchored just off the shore. This is particularly enjoyable when drinking *cremat*, a concoction made from rum and hot coffee that was also introduced by seamen who were employed on the Cuba run about 100 years ago.

Palamós, which has no direct link with either Llafranc or Calella, dates back to the thirteenth century, having been designated a royal port in 1279. It had to resist pirates, easterly winds and heavy seas that knocked down the early breakwaters almost as soon as they were built. However, it persisted and prospered, built up a thriving trade with the Americas after 1778, and then concentrated on the cork industry. By the latter half of the twentieth century it had modern buildings, hotels, restaurants and other holiday attractions.

Palamós has an enthusiastic sailing club with all the usual amenities but not much space for casual visitors due to the size of the fishing fleet. Pedaloes are available and there is a beach. Although this has coarse sand and shelves steeply, it has received a European blue flag award for its cleanliness. One of the port's best known annual events is the procession of the Virgin of the Carmelites on 16 July when the Mother and Child are carried through the streets in their own small boat which is almost invisible under its canopy of flowers. The town boasts a Museum of Local History in the Cau de la Costa Brava, while Calonge, slightly inland, has an Archaeological Museum housed in what remains of its ancient castle.

From Palamós a scenic route heads south along the coast to **Platja d'Aro**, a somewhat aggressively determined tourist resort, full of what are claimed to be the most modern and popular discos on the Costa Brava. It has hotels and restaurants of practically every description, from first class down to the typical seaside variety, augmented by a wide range of shops, neon signs and organised entertainments. The beaches are clean and attractive but they tend to be rather overcrowded during the season and the shore shelves quickly. Golfers can visit the Costa Brava Club at Santa Cristina d'Aro a short drive away. It has more or less the same amenities as its counterpart at Pals with the addition of a hotel next door that arranges temporary membership and the payment of green fees for its guests. There are several campsites, both locally and in the vicinity of Palamós, some of which provide bungalows as well. An added advantage is that at least three of them stay open right through the year.

In complete contrast **S'Agaró**, almost next door, is a comparatively sedate residential village which was planned for holidaymakers in 1924. It has a secluded luxury hotel that charges top prices, an

The busy marina at Sant Feliu de Guixols

attractive church and some well manicured gardens with impressive sea views but very little else to attract the crowds.

Sant Feliu de Guixols, only a short distance away, owes its existence to a Benedictine monastery founded there in the tenth century. Some archaeologists think that there may have been one or even more much earlier settlements on the site. So far nothing has been discovered to substantiate this theory apart from the Cova d'en Daina, an impressive megalith at Romanyà de la Selva, a few kilometres away on a minor road to Calonge.

During the Middle Ages Sant Feliu de Guixols was a thriving coastal town with a shipyard on the beach that built everything from frigates and schooners to brigantines and typical Catalan vessels known as *barques de mitjana* which operated up and down the coast. Later the community became involved in the cork industry when merchantmen would anchor a short distance from the shore while great barges plied backwards and forwards loaded with cargoes unless bad weather intervened. The breakwater was built in 1904 and today the installations include a commercial dock, a basin for the fishing fleet and a section devoted to pleasure craft. The promenade, laid out nearly 150 years ago, is one of the widest and certainly among the most attractive of any along the Catalan coast. It is crowded with visitors during the season when children divide their attention between the sea, the sand and a small engine standing on the grass nearby. There are two or three upmarket hotels and several smaller establishments as well as three campsites. An excellent variety of seafood is offered by the many restaurants on the promenade and the nearby Rambla.

For searchers after antiquity not a great deal remains of the ancient monastery apart from the Porta Ferrada, a large iron-covered door half hidden behind three horseshoe arches surmounted by a carved stone gallery, which is thought to have been the original entrance. The Torre del Fum and the Torre del Corn stand guard over the old church whose interior was considerably restored and updated during the fourteenth century and there are plans to rebuild some of the remaining fortifications. A small, serpentine road climbs up the wooded hillside above the Paseo Maritimo to the ancient hermitage of Sant Elm. It has been completely restored, and more often than not is firmly closed, but it is well worth going up there for the view. Other attractions include the small but atmospheric old quarter, the well patronised bullring and an occasional building, such as the Casino dels Nois, which is modern and colourful in the Art Nouveau style.

The delightful resort of **Tossa de Mar** endeared itself to animal lovers by officially banning bullfighting in 1989. The mayor also decided not to advertise similar events taking place in other centres, nor to allow the sale of any animals on the streets. It was a bold move which does not appear to have upset the local residents unduly, possibly because the town has a good many other things to offer instead. First and foremost it is linked to Sant Feliu de Guixols by a spectacular corniche; some 23km (14 miles) of convoluted roadway with frequent lay-bys where motorists can stop to admire the view. Sometimes it runs along the top of perpendicular cliffs while, at others, it plunges down to inspect enchanting little coves which are surrounded by oaks and pine trees. Each one has a descriptive name such as Bona Cove, providing a safe, though temporary, anchorage for pleasure craft, or L'Infern en Caixa (Hell's Coffin). The latter is surrounded by rocky islets that must have made even the most intrepid pirates think twice before putting ashore there.

Tossa de Mar is built round a sandy bay with a rocky promontory on either side. The medieval quarter, still partly protected by walls and towers and known as the Vila Vella, is at the southern end of the cove, spilling out into a jumble of narrow streets and old stone houses, inhabited mainly by fishermen and their families. It is also, very properly, the home of the Vila Vella Museum which, with a pleasing disregard for continuity, displays both prehistoric relics, with mosaics excavated from the Roman house nearby, and contemporary works of art including a painting by Chagall. The Vila Nova (New Town) continued to expand beyond the shadow of the twelfth-century walls, each new stage being described as modern in relation to everything that had been built before. However, compared with many Modernistic additions like the Casa Sans, the old section is archaic and extremely picturesque. Tossa is certainly colourful, due in part to the influence of artists like Marc Chagall and Metzinger who discovered its potential in the 1930s in the wake of their Spanish counterparts who had been painting there for years. There are plenty of hotels and apartment blocks, restaurants, campsites and attractive sandy beaches within easy reach. The sand is coarse and the beaches tend to be busy but Tossa has so far managed to avoid being overwhelmed by highrise tourist developments.

The same cannot be said for **Lloret de Mar** which is extremely proud of the fact that it is reputed to have as many hotels as Madrid sandwiched into a very small space. It is a package tour paradise, with discos, a clean and popular beach, bars and cafés and palm trees lining the promenade. Out of season it is much quieter. There is plenty of space to wander round the bay and visit the sanctuary of Santa Cristina with its ex-voto offerings, many of them model ships recalling the days when a handful of building yards provided most of the activity on the beach. It is a resort which is certainly never dull or totally deserted and, with some justification, has been called the Fun Capital of the Costa Brava.

Blanes, the southernmost port on the Costa Brava, was established by the Romans, who called it *Blanda*, and featured as a coastal settlement in the writings of Pomponio Mela in the first century AD. It was a busy maritime centre during the Middle Ages and had important boat construction yards turning out vessels along the seafront less than 100 years ago. Nowadays it is mildly industrial but concentrates mainly on fishing and keeping its many seasonal visitors happy. The resort is not overburdened with hotels and restaurants although there are more than enough highrise buildings all along the front. There is plenty of budget accommodation including

A panorama of Tossa de Mar

apartments and there are also campsites to provide for both tents and caravans. The beach is a good one but the shore shelves rapidly so it is not ideal for children. As far as yachtsmen are concerned, visitors' moorings are somewhat restricted but novices anxious to master the art of sailing or waterskiing can arrange for lessons at the appropriate local school. An added attraction for potential buyers is the used boat market which is held in May every year.

Blanes has surprisingly few tangible relics from the distant past apart from the nearby ruins of Blanes castle, the old fishermen's quarter of S'Auguer and the thirteenth-century church of Mare de Déu del Vilar. The latter has model ships under full sail suspended from the roof and some attractive artwork round the altar. Among the most popular local pastimes are a visit to the aquarium belonging to the Fish Research Institute and a stroll down to the fish market in the late afternoon when the day's catch is displayed for auction. However, neither quite compares with the two botanical gardens — the Mar i Murtra and the Pinya de Rosa — containing literally thousands of different Mediterranean and exotic plants which can be inspected at different times throughout the year. The outlying convent of Sant Francesco has an attractive little cove named after it, adding a further dimension to the series of beaches that extend as far as the mouth of the Río Tordera.

From Blanes a secondary road makes a brief sortie into the province of Barcelona in order to join the N11 for a more or less straight run due north to Girona, the provincial capital some 43km (26 miles) away. There is nothing particularly memorable along this route although there are one or two side options for motorists with plenty of time to spare. For example, **Caldes de Malavella**, reached along a minor road off to the right, is a spa town whose hot springs were well known to the Romans. They were modernised and updated at the end of the nineteenth century when the Vichy Catala, standing in its own park, was given a slightly Moorish appearance.

Alternatively, a choice of small scenic byways, exploring the countryside to the west of the main road, call at places like Hostalric, crouching behind the remains of its ancient walls, and Breda, in the foothills of the Sierra de Montseny, where the major occupation is making pottery. Further to the north, Santa Coloma de Farners has the remnants of a twelfth-century castle and a circular route along two nearby river valleys, calling at Sant Hilari Sacalm and Anglès before joining the Río Ter for an easy run into **Girona**.

The capital is one of the showplaces of Catalunya, as long as you ignore the industrial developments spread out along the river banks and concentrate on the ancient heart of this City of a Thousand Sieges. From being a well fortified Iberian settlement and an important Roman stronghold on the Via Augusta, it became the focal point of one of the great Catalan earldoms during the Middle Ages. Because of its strategic position on the route to Barcelona, repeated attempts were made to capture it. The Visigoths were there and so were the Jews and the Arabs. The 'Song of Roland' immortalises an assault by Charlemagne, while in 1809 the city held out for more than 7 months against 35,000 Napoleonic troops until it was literally starved into submission. Everywhere in the ancient quarter there are reminders of its various inhabitants but nowhere is this more apparent than in the Call, a terraced area of dark twisting alleys and sombre stone houses where the first Hebrew families lived in AD889.

Originally the Jewish community, or *aljama*, came under the direct protection of the crown and in return paid regular financial tributes and kept an eye on the City Fathers. This gave the sovereign of the day an excellent opportunity to meddle in various local affairs. The community, one of the most influential in Spain, had its own laws and customs and was an important religious centre, especially in the early thirteenth century. This was when Moses Ben Nahmen, as Grand Rabbi of Catalunya, introduced the Càbala, a theosophical movement which was to have far reaching consequences. This state of affairs caused a great deal of resentment. Before long all the entrances to the Call along the Carrer de la Força were sealed off because the Catholics maintained that the Jews were upsetting their Christian activities. Then a dawn to dusk curfew was imposed, anti-Semitism flourished under the expert guidance of the Inquisition and the area rapidly degenerated into a ghetto.

Many of the families moved out of their own accord, leaving the remainder to be expelled in 1492, the same year that the Moors were finally ousted from their last remaining toehold in Granada. Part of the Call was redeveloped during the Middle Ages but a large percentage was left to its own devices until 1983 when the authorities decided to clean up the whole area and preserve it as an historic entity. It is a fascinating district to explore with its innumerable steps, gloomy sunless passages, secluded patios and tall, brooding houses, some with empty niches that once held the sacred scrolls.

The Carrer de la Força, where much of the trouble started, follows the path of the Via Augusta to the attractive Plaça de la Catedral which is ideally placed for sightseeing in the ancient sector. A majestic stairway with nearly 100 shallow stone steps leads up to the cathedral, built in the fourteenth and fifteenth centuries on the site of a much older church. It was originally planned along conventional lines but in 1386, and again in 1416, meetings of Catalunya's leading architects agreed, somewhat reluctantly, to do away with the idea of three aisles in order to provide more light and a greater feeling of spaciousness. The result is the widest single Gothic nave in Europe, measuring 23m (75ft) across with very little decoration apart from the many stained-glass windows and a magnificent silver and enamel altarpiece under a matching canopy. The twelfth-century cloister, with its double line of columns, has some fine stone carving as well as a slightly more recent group of sculptures, the Mare de Déu de Bell Ull, by Master Bartomeu.

The cathedral treasures, kept in the adjoining Museu Capitular de la Catedral — MCCG for short — are compulsive viewing and should certainly not be missed. One of the most memorable items is the Tapestry of the Creation, dating from the early twelfth century. It shows Christ as the centre of the universe surrounded by Adam and Eve, prehistoric and fanciful wildlife of every description, the four winds and a framework of squares roughly tracing the development of mankind. There are also beautifully embroidered altar fronts, gold and silver plate, paintings, sculptures, caskets and ancient manuscripts. These include a bible that once belonged to the French king Charles V and an illustrated Baetus Commentary on the Apocalypse which has been in existence for more than 1,000 years.

The Museu d'Art de Girona, in the former Episcopal Palace next door to the cathedral, also collects altar pieces in addition to other items of sacred art. It has some unique exhibits such as the amusing beam from Cruïlles as well as a reliquary and a small silver altar, designed to be carried about, which once belonged to Sant Pere de Rodes. There are also paintings, statues and murals, gold and silverware, an extremely rare glassmaker's table from the fourteenth century but so far not a great deal in the way of contemporary art.

On one side of the steps leading up to the cathedral is a fifteenth-century mansion known as the Pia Almoina which looks rather formidable but was, in fact, much given to good works towards the end of the Middle Ages. On the opposite side, the Portal Sobreportas, with its sturdy, round towers, was part of the original defences. It was a sort of upmarket guard house from which one of the local nobility kept a constant lookout for the least sign of trouble on the far bank of the river. It is also reputed to be the gate through which anyone condemned to death was led out for execution.

For some reason the nearby church of Sant Feliu was built outside the ramparts. According to some accounts it was once part of a monastery but other sources maintain that it marks the site of an ancient cemetery where the martyred Sant Narcís, an early Bishop of Girona, and Sant Feliu were buried. Whichever version is correct, Sant Narcís was provided with a worthy tomb in the fourteenth century while a number of early Christian sarcophagi were preserved in the chancel, despite the fact that some of their carvings owed more to mythology than to the New Testament.

Other places of interest in the vicinity include the so-called Arab Baths, modelled on Roman lines with a hot room, a steam area, a tepid section and a cold pool surrounded by columns. Nearby is the little church of Sant Nicolau, once attached to the monastery of Sant Pere de Galligants which is now the home of the city's Archaeologi-

*Girona — the
Arab Baths*

*Opposite: Girona
cathedral*

cal Museum. It is particularly interested in prehistoric and Iberian relics, Roman art and Jewish memorial plaques and headstones, augmented by a variety of other items discovered in the surrounding area. Slightly further afield are the Torre Gironella, the convent of Sant Dominenec whose church was also given a single nave, the sparse remains of the ancient university and the attractive Palau dels Aguillana. From here it is only a stone's throw to the Carrer del Ciutadans, an elegant thoroughfare in medieval times when it was lined with impressive mansions like the much restored Fontana D'Or and the Casa de la Ciutat on the Plaça del Vi.

Girona also has its modern attractions, including the unusual Farinera Teixidor, a flour mill built in 1910 which is still very much in business, and the Casa de la Punxa on the Calle de Santa Eugènia. This is slightly more recent and has a turret decorated in green ceramics. The local poet and architect, Rafael Masó, was largely responsible for introducing twentieth-century colour combinations, tiles, ironwork and sculptures to the city and this has resulted in some nice touches such as eight yellow ceramic owls nesting above the façade of the Casa Batlle on the Calle Nou, near the town hall.

Regardless of all its many attractions, and the fact that it has its own airport and regular train and bus services, Girona is inexplicably short of hotels, with nothing at all in the luxury bracket. Its shops and restaurants are unremarkable and there are few open spaces with the exception of the Plaça de Catalunya, built over a short stretch of the Río Onyar, and the attractive Parque de la Devisa just on the outskirts. However, it is possible to find somewhere to stay in the old quarter, or on the N11 on the way to either Figueres or Barcelona, or find a comfortable base in one of the many coastal resorts.

Surprisingly few visitors bother to explore the countryside to the west of Girona and this is a pity because there are some really delightful small towns and villages as well as historic buildings and attractive scenery. A case in point is **Banyoles** in the Garrotxa mountains to the north. It is an atmospheric little place on the shores of a large lake and owes its existence to the ancient monastery of Sant Esteve. Its antique attractions include an arcaded thirteenth-century square, the church of Santa Maria dels Turers (built at about the same time) and the Pia Almoina with a very viewable cloister and an archaeological museum. It is well on the way to becoming a popular holiday resort, especially with fishermen in search of carp, and water sports enthusiasts who practise regularly for the well publicised contest held there every year. There are two small *hostales* near the lake, one of which has a restaurant and a swimming pool. Both *hostales* have rooms with private baths. There are also two campsites quite close by. It is possible to drive or walk right around the water's edge, calling at Porqueres in order to inspect the twelfth-century church of Santa Maria. The most noticeable things about the church are the doorway with its triple arches and some unusual carvings on the capitals of a triumphal arch just inside.

From Banyoles the C150 calls briefly at Serinyà, with its modest but undoubtedly prehistoric cave paintings, on the way to **Besalú**. This is a small medieval gem on the banks of the Río Fluvià which, for a brief period during the Middle Ages, was the capital of an earldom that extended from Figueres to the valley of the Río Ter. In due course it was taken over by the lords of Barcelona, after which it made no further attempt to move with the times.

The town's most outstanding feature is an oddly shaped fortified bridge with a sharp bend in the middle protected by an octagonal tower. It was built in the fourteenth century on considerably older foundations and has now been carefully restored. Beyond a second defensive tower at the far end is a cluster of buildings, many of which

look much as they did in the twelfth and thirteenth centuries. The
church of Sant Pere de Besalú, all that remains of the old Benedictine
monastery, is easily identified by the two rather mischievous looking
lions keeping watch over a carved window above the door. The
church of Santa Julià was once part of a hospital whereas the *mikwà*,
used by the Jews for ritual ablutions, is said to be the only example
of its kind in Spain and one of the very few to be seen anywhere in
Europe. Other places of interest include the Gothic church of Sant
Vicenç, some ruins, a number of medieval houses and an attractive
little square surrounded by its original arcades.

Most of the villages to the north and east of Besalú have something
to offer people in search of early churches. **Beuda** not only provides
a twelfth-century version with a decorative font but also the large,
severe El Sant Sepulcre de Palera nearby which was part of an early
monastery. **Navata**, on the road to Figueres, has an old parish church,
notable mainly for its stone carvings, iron work and just a trace of
mural paintings, while **Lladó** goes one better, having preserved a
few remains of the Augustine monastery of Santa María.

Visitors in search of unusual scenery as opposed to ecclesiastical
relics would do better to head westwards into the Parc Natural de la
Zona Volcànica de la Garrotxa, also known as the Olot Volcanic
Zone. It is a varied and extremely fascinating area, divided up
roughly between woods and farmlands with about thirty probably
extinct volcanoes, some ancient lava flows and little marshy patches
to the south of Olot that once extended along several of the nearby
valleys. Apart from La Pedra del Diable, or Devil's Stone, to the east
of Sant Pau, there are no menhirs or dolmens left behind by the
prehistoric inhabitants and even some of the medieval villages were
badly damaged or destroyed by a series of earthquakes in 1427, 1428
and 1430. However, the local communities picked themselves up
and continued to plant crops, raise cattle, occupy isolated farmhouses and use lava blocks to build low walls and little shelters that
look like gigantic beehives. Some of the ninth-century hamlets
developed into villages or smallish towns, a few castles and bridges
were built and artists came to the region, attracted by its colours and
unusual landscapes.

As long ago as 1917, plans were put forward to give some form of
protection to the region but it was not until a cinder quarry began to
encroach on one of the most attractive areas near El Croscat that the
general outcry led to official action. In 1982 the volcanic zone was
declared a site of national interest with some attendant geological
and botanical reserves, to be followed 3 years later by the creation of

Medieval Besalú — the church of Sant Pere de Besalú

the present nature park.

As with other parks in Catalunya, adequate arrangements were made for visitors but at the same time certain rules and regulations were laid down. No-one is allowed to camp in the reserves but special sites are provided in open country, in addition to hotels and hostels in a few of the villages. The network of paths is well signposted, jeeps and motor cycles must not deviate from the roads and cycle tracks and there are car parks at strategic intervals. Picking flowers, uprooting plants, collecting rocks and killing or catching any of the wildlife is strictly forbidden and everyone must be reasonably quiet and take any litter home with them. There are regular bus services between Olot and half a dozen heighbouring centres like Girona, Vic and Figueres. In addition, taxis can be hired in Olot and guides are available from the Casal dels Volcans in the Avenida de Santa Coloma.

There are only two or three main roads and a few minor ones for motorists who want to see as much as possible without having to walk too far. With this in mind, the C150 from Besalú calls at **Castellfollit de la Roca**, poised along the edge of a basalt cliff over-looking the Fluvià and Turonell rivers with the church of Sant Salvador clinging grimly to the far end of the crag. From here the road heads south towards Olot, passing a campsite on the way, while a secondary route branches off almost immediately to Sant Joan les Fonts and La Canya. Further to the south the GE524 from Banyoles makes straight for **Sant Pau**, a fortified medieval village with an ancient baronial hall and a picturesque old quarter round the arcaded Plaça del Firal dels Bous. There are also two small churches and some fairly basic accommodation for people who decide to explore the surrounding countryside on foot.

Beyond Sant Pau the road passes quite close to the wooded slopes of Santa Margarida volcano, the largest of them all, with a well defined crater that blew its top with tremendous energy but left the rest of the cone intact. El Croscat, on the opposite side of the road, is said to have been the last to erupt, 11,500 years ago. Slightly further on are the beech woods of Jordà with a poem by Joan Maragall carved on a pillar near the entrance. The region is also full of oaks, with some alder groves and hazel trees along the river banks and patches of aspen, chestnuts and pines. The main animals to look out for are wild cats, badgers, shrews and dormice with perhaps an occasional otter or wild boar. Lizards and vipers live in the volcanic crevices while the birdlife is extremely varied, consisting of well over 100 different species from eagles and falcons to great spotted woodpeckers, owls, finches and marsh tits.

Olot, the local capital, is a colour-conscious centre and this is largely due to the school of landscape artists established there 200 years ago. The Museu Comarcal de la Garrotxa has a bit of every-thing, dabbling in ethnology and local history but visited chiefly for its extensive collection of Catalan art. There are pictures and sculptures by early members of the school, sections devoted to furniture and ceramics and wood carvings including little painted religious figures which are still made by local craftsmen and make attractive souvenirs.

Among several buildings that are worth seeing are the Casa Sola Morales with its wrought iron balconies, eye-catching stone figures and decorative carvings, and the Casa Masramon, said to be one of Rafael Masó's most outstanding works. In addition to a sprinkling of small hotels and *hostales*, including a youth hostel, there are some typical little restaurants. A variety of training courses are available, as well as frequent exhibitions and a wealth of information obtain-able from the elegant Casal dels Volcans and the tourist office off the Plaça del Mercat.

One of the best views of the volcanic basin round Olot is from the road to Sant Joan de les Abadesses, an old town which has been overtaken by industry following the discovery of coal in the area. The village originally grew up round an abbey founded by Guifre the Hairy, whose daughter Emma was the first abbess. The present church of Sant Joan was consecrated 200 years later, in 1150, but part of it was later destroyed in an earthquake. It has some interesting and unusual possessions, acquired in its younger days, and a delightful cloister dating from the fifteenth century. From here there is an alternative though poorly surfaced route back to Olot, or a much easier and shorter drive to the Pyrénean town of **Ripoll**. It is worth visiting for the remains of its former monastery of Santa María, much of which was destroyed by fire in 1835, and because it is on the scenic N152 that runs due south to Vic and on to Barcelona.

Additional Information

Places of Interest

Blanes
Aquarium
For viewing times enquire at the Tourist Office (see below for telephone number).

Botanical Gardens
Open: 9am-6pm April to October. Otherwise 10am-5pm. Closed Saturday, Sunday and holiday mornings, Christmas Day and 1 and 6 January.

El Port de la Selva
Monastery of Sant Pere de Rodes
Above El Port de la Selva
Open: normally 10am-2pm and 4pm to sundown.

Empúries
Greek and Roman Ruins
Near L'Escala
Open: 10am-2pm and 3-7pm spring and summer, 10am-2pm and 3-5pm autumn and winter.
☎ 972 77 02 08

Figueres
Teatro-Museu Dali
Pujada Castel, on the way to the castle. Open: 10.30am-1pm and 3.30-7pm Tuesday to Sunday. Closed 1 January and 25 December.

Girona
Museu Capitular de la Catedral
Open: normally 10am-1.30pm and 3.30 to 6.30pm. Closed in the afternoon from November to February. May be open at lunch-time at the height of the season. The entry ticket includes the cloister.

Archaeological Museum
Open: 10am-1pm and 4.30-7pm. Closed Monday and some Sunday afternoons.

Arab Baths
Open: 10am-1pm and 4.30-7pm. Closed Monday and sometimes in the afternoon out of season.

Museu d'Art de Girona
Open: 10am-1pm and 4.30-7pm. Closed Monday and sometimes in the afternoon out of season.

Olot Volcanic Zone
Casal dels Volcans
Av. de Santa Coloma
Olot ☎ 972 26 62 02
Also Sant Pau
Can Vayreda Tourist Office
☎ 972 68 03 49

Palafrugell
Cape Roig Botanical Gardens
Near Palafrugell
Conducted tours 9am-9pm in summer, 9am-6pm in winter.

Parc Natural dels Aiguamolls de l'Empordà
Information Centre
El Cortalet
Castello d'Empúries, on the road to
Sant Pere Pescador
☎ 972 25 03 22

Tourist Offices

Banyoles
Passeig de la Indústria 25
☎ 972 57 55 73

Begur
Av. Onze de Setembre
☎ 972 62 34 79

Besalú
Plaça de la Llibertat 1
☎ 972 59 02 25 (June to October)

Blanes
Plaça Catalunya
☎ 972 33 03 48

Cadaqués
Cotxe 2A
☎ 972 25 83 15

L'Escala
Plaça de les Escoles 1
☎ 972 77 06 03

L'Estartit
Passeig Maritim 47
☎ 972 75 89 10

Figueres
Plaça del Sol
☎ 972 50 31 55

Girona
Rambla Llibertat 1
☎ 972 20 26 79

Lloret de Mar
Plaça de la Vila
☎ 972 36 47 35

Olot
Mulleres, Plaça del Mercat
☎ 972 26 01 41

Palafrugell
Carrilet 2
☎ 972 30 02 28

Palamós
Passeig del Mar 8
☎ 972 31 43 90

Pals
Plaça d'Espanya 7
☎ 972 63 61 61 (July to September)

Platja d'Aro
Carrer Verdaguer 11
☎ 972 81 71 79

Roses
Avinguda de Rhode
☎ 972 25 73 31

Sant Feliu de Guixols
Plaça d'Espanya 6-9
☎ 972 32 03 80

Tossa de Mar
Carretera de Lloret
☎ 972 34 01 08

2

COSTA DEL MARESME

S outh of Blanes, where the Costa del Maresme takes over from the
Costa Brava, the shoreline undergoes a spectacular change. The
rugged cliffs and isolated little coves disappear, the hills retreat into
the distance and their place is taken by long, often wide and invariably sandy beaches that stretch, with an occasional interruption, to
the outer fringes of Barcelona. The N11 from the north joins the coast
near **Malgrat de Mar**, not far from the old castle ruins at Palafolls and
the 'Marineland', where performing dolphins entertain the crowds.
From here the road keeps company with the Mediterranean, calling
at Calella whose highrise apartment blocks, interspersed with a few
hotels, are separated from the water by a tree-lined promenade. It
also has a lighthouse built on a small rocky promontory, beyond
which are one or two small resorts on the way to **Arenys de Mar**.

This busy and quite historic little port is fairly spread out, rather
than concentrated along the foreshore, and divides its attention more
or less equally between fishing and the tourist industry. In the past,
half the population earned a living from the sea. They were either
sailors or boat-builders, employed in one of the allied trades or had
business interests in places as far afield as Mexico or Venezuela
where the Spanish merchantmen called in at regular intervals. When
steel hulls replaced wooden ones and sails gave way to steam,
Arenys de Mar was forced to adopt a new way of life. Today the
fishing fleet, numbering about 100 boats in all, lands around 7,000
tons of fish a year and the evening auctions attract large crowds of
holidaymakers as well as buyers from all over the surrounding area.
Apart from the usual accommodation there are four local campsites,
a large number of restaurants and facilities for a wide range of water
sports. Other attractions include the Frederic Marés Lacemaking

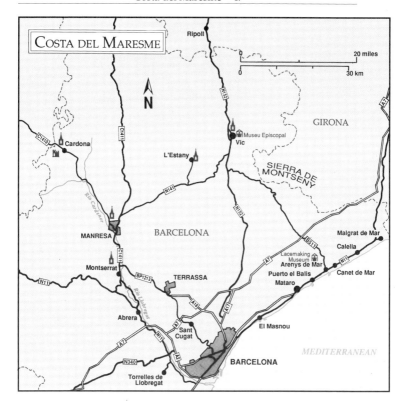

Museum, the church of Santa María with its fine Baroque altarpiece
and some modern sculptures by Josep Llimona in the cemetery.

For motorists who would welcome a change of scenery, the B511
provides a link with the Sierra de Montseny on the far side of the
motorway. However, anyone who prefers to do their sightseeing on
foot would be well advised to join the GR5 at Canet de Mar, just next
door. It sets off resolutely through strawberry fields, climbs up into
the mountains of the Montseny Nature Park, joins the GR2 from the
Pyrénées, and bypasses Barcelona to arrive eventually at Sitges, on
the Costa Daurada. On the other hand, it also meets the GR92 near
Sant Martí de Montnegre. This Grand Randonnée, which has already
inspected the Costa Brava, takes things a bit more easily across the
lowlands of the Costa del Maresme, past the Iberian settlement of
Puig Castellar and up into the Collserola mountain range for a
panoramic view of Barcelona.

About the same distance from Arenys de Mar, in the opposite direction, is **Caldes d'Estrac**. This is a pretty, little warm water spa that once rivalled Sitges in the affections of English holidaymakers and acknowledges the fact by calling its attractive promenade El Passeig dels Anglesos. It is companionably close to **Puerto el Balis**, built more recently with plenty of berths for pleasure craft and all the modern amenities, as well as a sailing school and tuition for would-be waterskiers. An added attraction is the nearby Club de Golf Llavaneres, one of the smallest in Spain. Its nine holes are quite demanding and the restaurant specialises in a wide range of traditional dishes. **Mataro** was once the capital of a maritime province although, for the moment at least, it is only a minor local holiday resort. However, it has some Roman remains and one or two choice examples of Art Nouveau, such as the Casa Coll i Regàs on the Carrer d'Argentona. After this, the N11 calls in at El Masnou with its small municipal museum, before dashing headlong into the old Roman town of Badalona, and losing itself in the industrial wastes on the outskirts of Barcelona.

BARCELONA
In order to appreciate all the different facets of this exceptional city it is as well to know a little about its background, covering something over 2,000 years. It began as the Iberian town of *Laye*, on an unassuming little hill called Mons Taber, but was overrun in the third century BC by the Carthaginians and renamed *Barcino* in honour of their ruler Hamilcar Barca. He was succeeded by his son Hannibal who, after a number of early successes against the Roman legions, was finally defeated and poisoned himself in 183BC to avoid being taken prisoner. Once in control, the Romans established a colony of their own on Mons Taber but it was not until the third century AD that they surrounded it with massive walls, some of which are still standing. Despite all these precautions, it was captured first by the Visigoths, then by the Moors and finally by the Franks under Charlemagne. At last, with the approval of Guifré the Hairy, it became the capital of the powerful earldom of Barcelona. In 1137 Ramon Berenguer IV, the Count of Barcelona, married Petronila, heir to the House of Aragon, thereby uniting Catalunya and Aragon under one crown.

Jaume I, generally regarded as Catalunya's greatest king, not only recaptured Valencia and the Balearic Islands from the Arabs but also created a number of basic institutions such as the Council of One Hundred for the city, the Maritime Consulate and the Corts

Catalanes. In 1438 Barcelona received a charter from Alfons the Magnanimous authorising it to build a harbour of its own. After this he left for Naples and the Generalitat decided that it had had enough of monarchs and deposed his heir, Joan II.

Obtaining permission to build a port was one thing, constructing it was quite another. Because of high seas, shifting sands and a number of serious political upheavals, it proved to be a long and tedious job. Nevertheless, Barcelona continued to grow in both size and importance, consolidating its position as a major European port, a cosmopolitan city full of colour and variety. The city restored and expanded its ancient university, encouraged music in all its different forms and threw itself gleefully into the remarkable world of Art Nouveau with the help of architects like Antoni Gaudí. It staged two great international exhibitions, in 1888 and 1929, and even managed to survive Franco's displeasure after providing a refuge for the Republican Government during the Civil War before being captured by the Nationalists in January 1939.

Despite its thoroughly modern outlook, Barcelona celebrates as often and as enthusiastically as any other place in Spain. In September giant figures, usually representing medieval kings and queens, are brought into the city from all over Catalunya to take part in processions in honour of Our Lady of Mercy, or La Merced. *L'ou com balla* — 'the dancing egg' — is part of the Corpus Christi festival, said to have been introduced in Barcelona and Girona during the fourteenth century and taken up soon afterwards by Valencia, Lleida, Sevilla and Toledo. Legend has it that it all started in Liège where a nun called Juliana had a peculiar vision whenever she began to pray. It took the form of a full moon with a shadow in the middle. She said that eventually Christ revealed to her that the circle represented all the liturgical celebrations marred by the fact that there was nothing dedicated to His presence in the Eucharist.

In 1246 a synod called by Roberto de Torote, the Bishop of Liège, officially recognised a special feast day and 19 years later Urbano IV issued a Papal Bull setting a permanent date for Corpus Christi. John XXII went even further when he ordered that the Body of Christ should be carried in solemn procession, after which the Host in its magnificent monstrance was the focal point of all the festivities. As well as several other religious occasions, there are many less traditional but equally well attended events ranging from operas, theatres and concerts to fairs, exhibitions and sporting fixtures held at frequent intervals throughout the year.

There is so much to see in Barcelona that it is always difficult to

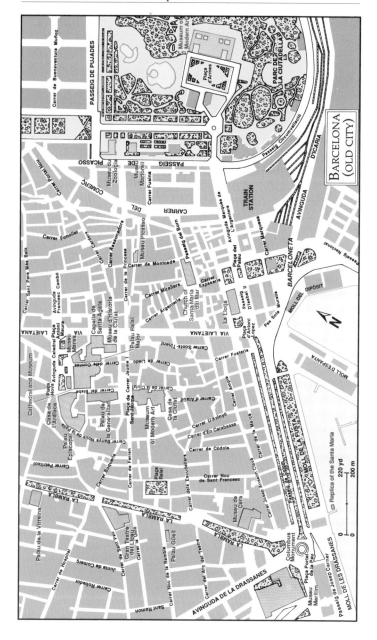

BARCELONA (OLD CITY)

The skyline of Barcelona

decide exactly where to begin. It is essentially a personal decision because, unlike so many other centres, the places of interest cover a wide area and some form of transport, either private or public, is essential in order to inspect them all. There is a fast and inexpensive metro, plenty of buses advertising their routes with timetables at nearly every stop and taxis are very reasonable but may be held up in the inevitable traffic jams. Parking is far from easy, even during the low season, so anyone who finds an empty space would do well to leave the car there for as long as possible.

Visitors who favour the area-by-area approach would probably start in the Barri Gòtic, or Gothic Quarter, following the example of the earliest inhabitants. There is certainly nothing Iberian about it these days, and even the few Roman remains have been altered considerably. However, Mons Taber is still there, crowned with a splendid Gothic cathedral. It was originally the site of a temple to Augustus, four of whose columns are preserved in the Centre Excursionista de Catalunya on the nearby Carrer Paradis.

The logical starting point for a tour of what was once known as the cathedral quarter is the Plaça Nova at the end of the Avinguda Catedral. The first ancient landmarks to be seen are two Roman towers that once guarded the western entrance to the city, but they were adapted to requirements in the twelfth century and incorporated into the adjoining buildings. On one side is the Palau Episcopal and on the other the Casa de l'Ardiaca, built into the ancient walls as a home for the archdeacon but used these days to house the city archives. Just next door, on the left, is the Plaça de la Seu, a little square overlooked by the cathedral. It is a favourite meeting place for wandering musicians of various nationalities and townspeople who congregate there on Saturdays and Sundays to join in the ancient folk dance, or *sardana*.

The present cathedral is the third to occupy the site, replacing a Romanesque church during the fourteenth and fifteenth centuries, although the façade was only completed about 100 years ago. It is just as impressive inside as out; spacious, very well lit and full of fascinating details. The great sweep of the nave is cut off in its prime by the chancel but this is so viewable in its own right that it proves to be an asset rather than a liability. The choir stalls are beautifully carved and decorated with coats-of-arms belonging to the Knights of the Golden Fleece who were summoned there in the early 1600s by Charles I in his capacity as the Holy Roman Emperor Charles V. The aisles on either side are lined with chapels (some thirty in all), tombs such as those of Ramòn Berenguer and his wife Almodis, painted altarpieces and other historic items. Below the high altar is the crypt of Santa Eulàlia where an alabaster sarcophagus contains the relics of this martyred virgin who was a native of Barcelona and is the city's patron saint.

The cloister, with its chapels, arches, carvings and iron work, is also well worth seeing. One of the bays is dedicated to St George, shown in the act of killing the dragon. Also look out for the fifteenth-century fountain, where an empty eggshell is balanced unsteadily on a jet of water during Corpus Christi for the annual *l'ou com balla*. Among the cathedral treasures is the splendidly ornate monstrance, glittering with gem stones and standing in the sacristy on a silver chair known as the Cadira del Rei Martí. Other articles of religious significance are housed in the small museum.

Another imposing building, this time facing the enclosed Plaça del Rei beyond the cathedral, is the Palau Reial Major, once the home of the Counts of Barcelona who also became the Kings of Aragon. An unusual corner staircase leads up to the Saló del Tinell, a great hall with six massive stone arches which was only started in 1359 after astrologists were called in to advise on the most auspicious date for laying the foundation stone. It has been the setting for many historic events but the claim that it is where the Catholic Monarchs, Ferdinand and Isabel, received Columbus on his return from San Salvador would appear to be wishful thinking and not proven fact.

Adjoining the unquestionably austere palace is the equally under-stated Capella de Santa Agata. Its main features are a beautiful wooden ceiling and Jaume Huguet's famous El Conestable altarpiece, commissioned by Peter of Portugal who is said to be the king shown on the centre panel. Also overlooking the Plaça del Rei are the Palau del Lloctinent, filled with the archives of the Crown of Aragon, some of which date back to the ninth century, and the Museu d'Historia de la Ciutat which concerns itself exclusively with the history of Barcelona. This is amply illustrated with archaeological discoveries, documents, maps and dozens of other items that have a direct bearing on the subject.

On the opposite side of the old palace gardens, on the Carrer de los Comtes, a line of very superior outhouses has been turned into the Museu Marés. It consists of an extraordinary conglomeration of exhibits which obviously appealed to the sculptor Frederic Marés' unusually varied tastes. There are stone carvings left by the Romans and later by the Arabs; medieval wooden sculptures, some of them distinctly over-painted; a typical Danse Macabre; baby-faced Madonnas and a sixteenth-century Entombment. In lighter vein, the upper halls are crammed with inconsequential and largely unrelated items like cigarette cards, scissors, little toy figures, decorative fans, clay pipes and even outsized cigars.

At the other end of this medieval complex is the Plaça de Sant Jaume which used to be the site of the Roman forum. On one side is the Palau de la Generalitat, the seat of the Catalan Government at various times since it was built in the early fifteenth century. It is open to view on Sunday mornings and is worth including for a number of different reasons. Not least of these are the Gothic stairway, leading to the elegant Gallery of Columns, and the Capilla de Sant Jordi with its embroideries and a silver statuette of the saint, better known in England as St George, who is also patron saint of Catalunya. Equally historic is the Casa de la Ciutat across the square, occupied by Sant Jaume's Council of One Hundred for more than three centuries and now the home of its successor, the City Council. It contains several items of interest including the Saló de Las Cronicás with its gold murals by the painter Josep Sert. Finally, out of sight but not out of mind, archaeologists have discovered a tracery of ancient streets running underneath the Carrer de los Comtes. There are also the remains of a buried church dating back some 1,600 years to the time when the Visigoths conquered the Roman city of *Barcino* and established their own capital on Mons Taber.

Not far from the Plaça de Sant Jaume, at the far end of the Carrer de Ferran, are the famous Ramblas, connecting the port area with the Plaça de Catalunya. In Moorish times this winding thoroughfare was an unpredictable little river, rushing down to the sea during the rainy season but used as a convenient market place and general trading area at other times of the year. It was covered over in the fourteenth century when the city found that it needed more space and transferred several institutions into newly constructed buildings outside the ancient walls. Over the next 500 years or so it gradually developed into an elongated promenade, with a walkway down the middle and narrow streets on either side, shaded by plane trees. Today it consists of five different sections, each with its own individual character. However, all of them are peppered with stalls of various descriptions, sandwiched in between long lines of buildings. Because the Ramblas are invariably crowded with sightseers they are also the haunt of petty criminals such as pickpockets, confidence tricksters and an occasional mugger. It is not a good idea to wander about wearing expensive jewellery, or carry a wallet full of money or a bulging handbag. It is far better to leave anything valuable in the hotel safe and only take the minimum

Locals enjoying the sardana *outside Barcelona cathedral*

amount of spending money.

As several of the hotels are located close to the large and most attractive Plaça de Catalunya, which incidentally is also well served by underground trains, it is the obvious place from which to set out for a lengthy stroll, beginning on the Rambla de Canaletes. This provides an ideal introduction with its ancient fountain where, according to local tradition, anyone who drinks the water will return to Barcelona. It is lined with stalls full of books and magazines which can usually be relied on to have something for people of every nationality. Before long this section blends into the Rambla dels Estudis, the site of the city's first university which moved to new premises in 1714. Nowadays the main attractions are stalls selling cage birds and a variety of small animals.

Number three on the list is the Rambla de Sant Josep, better known as the Rambla de les Flors. It has all the atmosphere of an open-air market because the majority of stands, often shaded by colourful umbrellas, are half hidden behind large jars and buckets filled to capacity with flowers and sprigs of greenery. Some visitors take a diversion here, wandering down the Carrer de la Portaferrissa to see what the fashion shops have to offer. Others prefer to visit the Palau de la Virreina where there are three museums to choose from and sometimes a temporary exhibition as well. As well as a small postal museum, there is the Cambo Collection, almost entirely made up of little-known works by world famous artists like Goya, Murillo, Zurbarán and El Greco. Italy is represented by painters such as Botticelli, Raphael, Tintoretto and Titian; there are Dutch masters of the calibre of Rubens and Van Dyck (the latter settled in England to become court painter during the reign of Charles I); while Fragonard provides some French interest. By way of contrast, the Museum of Decorative Arts is full of exhibits such as glass and ceramics, vases, clocks, figurines and some pleasing old tapestries. Slightly further on is the covered fruit and vegetable market, generally referred to as La Boqueria.

Beyond the Plaça de la Boqueria the name changes once again to become the Rambla dels Caputxins. Although it is liberally sprinkled with bars and restaurants, most of the attention is focused on the Gran Teatre del Liceu, one of the world's truly grand opera houses; a fact which is not immediately apparent from the outside. It has five magnificent, semi-circular balconies and is splendidly decorated, very much in keeping with the Wagnerian operas which have drawn large crowds ever since it was founded in 1847. The surrounding area was once a busy theatreland but the only example that has survived is the Teatro Principal, now definitely looking its age. Other nearby attractions include the Plaça Reial, once the site of a Capuchin convent, which is paved, planted with tall palm trees and surrounded by identical buildings, arcades and little bars. It has a fountain and street lights designed by Gaudí and is a popular meeting place which becomes even more crowded on Sunday mornings with coin and stamp collectors anxious to find something to buy or exchange at the market. The square is connected to the Rambla by the Carrer de Colom.

More or less opposite the square, across the Rambla in the Carrer Nou de la Rambla, the Museu del Teatre is housed in Gaudí's typical Palau Güell. It was built in the 1880s as a private, if palatial, residence with a vaulted basement for the horses and a roof whose eighteen chimneys and ventilation pipes wear an assortment of highly imaginative little cowls. Between the two, connected by a large vertical shaft with a dome on top, every floor and nearly every room has its own distinctive quality. There are marble columns, a variety of arches, ceilings covered in wood panels, iron work, paintings, inlaid ivory and unusual furniture that blends in perfectly with its surroundings.

The fifth and final Rambla, the Rambla de Santa Mònica, is generally considered to be the least attractive of them all. There is little or nothing to pause for along the way apart from some waxworks in the Museu de Cera on the left hand side. This is only about a block away from the Plaça Portal de la Pau, dominated by the towering and much decorated monument to Christopher Columbus who stands on top, pointing imperiously out to sea. It was built for the exhibition of 1888 and has a lift up to the viewing platform where there is an excellent view of both the port and the city.

Les Drassanes are located on the Passeig de Josep Carner, which Columbus could see if he glanced down over his right shoulder. They were the original shipyards, completed in the fourteenth century, and were essentially functional, consisting of long, parallel halls supported by arches and facing the waterfront. Having been expertly restored, they are the largest and best preserved of their kind still in existence and make a fitting background for the Museu Marítim. Anyone interested in ships and other nautical matters will find this museum totally fascinating. There are medieval maps and documents, including the Llibro del Consulat del Mar, the world's first maritime code, as well as figureheads, sea chests, navigating instruments, cannons, and models of naval craft and merchantmen. One of the most eye-catching items on display is a reproduction of the *Real*, Don Juan of Austria's flagship at the Battle of Lepanto in 1571. It was the last great naval engagement between galleys equipped with oars and resulted in a victory for the combined Spanish, Papal, Venetian and Genoese fleet which put an end to

Turkey as a maritime power. Adjoining Les Drassanes is a section of the medieval city walls, including the Portal de Santa Madrona, left standing when the rest were pulled down in 1854.

Below the Columbus monument, ferries known as *golondrinas* ply backwards and forwards across the harbour, crowded with sight-seers intent on getting a sailor's eye view of the foreshore. Among the sights to be seen is an exact replica of the *Santa Maria* in which Cristóbal Colón, as Columbus preferred to be called, sailed west-wards with the *Niña* and the *Pinta* in an effort to discover a sea route to India. Beyond it is the Moll de la Fusta, or ancient timber wharf, backed by a tree encrusted promenade. The latter has a clear view across to the marina on the Moll d'Espanya where visitors to the Reial Club Nàutic and the Reial Club Marítim can sometimes find a temporary berth. At the far end of the promenade, along the Passeig d'Isabel II, is the Plaça del Palau with its own reminders of the past including the old custom's house and La Llotja, built in 1380 and still doing service as the Barcelona stock exchange.

A block or two away is the fourteenth-century church of Santa María del Mar. This survived an earthquake in 1428 that damaged the great rose window, a bombardment in 1714 and a fire in 1936 but remains a masterpiece of Catalan Gothic architecture with fifteenth-century stained glass windows. In the past the congregation con-sisted mostly of sailors who lived in the district alongside wealthy families, many of whose mansions can still be seen on the Carrer de Montcada. The ones which attract the most attention are the Palau de Llio, where the Coleccion Rocamora consists mainly of costumes and accessories going back some 200 years, and the Palau Aguilar, the fifteenth-century mansion which is now the home of the Picasso Museum. It is not by any means the best or most representative collection of his works but is full of delightfully unexpected exam-ples, such as the drawings he did in Málaga when he was 8 years old, early etchings and engravings, portraits of his family and paintings from his famous Blue Period. Equally memorable are the studies for *Harlequin* and an incredible number of variations on the theme of *Las Meninas* by Velazques who was also considered to be a revolutionary painter in his day.

From the Plaça del Palau the Avinguda Marquès de l'Argentera heads straight for the Parc de la Ciutadella which has had an unpleasantly chequered history. When the city was overrun by Philip V in 1714 he demolished a large residential area in order to build a massive fortress. It was intended to be impregnable but was taken by the French without much effort less than 100 years later. In

Pedralbes Palace, built in the Italian Renaissance style, is now a museum

*The Gaudi
Museum,
Parc Güell*

1869 the whole building was presented to the people of Barcelona who knocked it down and replaced it with a spacious park. The result is an odd mixture of the past and the present, with the governor's palace and the arsenal left over from the fortress, a massive nineteenth-century Arc de Triomf, festooned with crowns, angels and coats-of-arms, and the Cascada, a monumental waterfall beside the boating lake. The Catalan Parliament shares the arsenal with the Museu d'Art Modern, although there are plans to move all the contents to the Museu d'Art de Catalan on Montjuïc. The exhibits are mostly from the late nineteenth and early twentieth centuries and cover a wide range from charcoal portraits, paintings and panels to sculptures, ceramics and furniture.

The Castell dels Tres Dragons is not as colourful as its name implies. It is large and square, built of red brick in 1888 and now the home of the Museu de Zoologia. The zoo itself, at the opposite end of the park, is considered by many people to be the best in Spain. As well as all the other animals, it has an aquarium, performing whales and dolphins and the only albino gorilla so far in captivity, who rejoices in the name of 'Snowflake'.

The Museu Martorell has sections on geology and natural history, while horticulturists will find much of interest in the greenhouses with their splendid array of plants and flowers. The neighbouring quarter of Barceloneta also has an aquarium on the Passeig Nacional and a seemingly endless number of narrow blocks of houses, occupied largely by fishermen and sailors. It is also full of cafés and restaurants that provide a wide range of delicious seafood dishes, sometimes accompanied by traditional and impromptu one-man serenades. The local beach is often crowded but there are many far more attractive places to choose for a swim.

In the latter half of the nineteenth century an extensive area surrounding the old city walls, which until then had been open country, was suddenly earmarked for development. Plans were drawn up on the grid system, calling for about 600 square blocks, with their corners shaved off, usually around six or seven storeys high and usually built with an open space in the middle. The ground floors were given over to shops and business premises of all descriptions with living quarters above them, while the rest of the buildings were divided up into apartments, some with their own private staircases. Art Nouveau, along with earlier forms of decoration, was very much in vogue and the area is full of attractive examples for anyone who has the time and determination to search for them. The plan was titled Reforma i Eixample (Renovation and enlargement) but this has been shortened to Eixample.

The Plaça de Catalunya is an easily identifiable meeting point between the old and the new, with the tree-lined Rambla de Catalunya heading straight for the Avinguda Diagonal, thereby dividing the area more or less down the middle. There are plenty of things to see on either side; beginning on the right, below the Plaça Urquinaona, just off the Via Laietana, with the Palau de la Música Catalana. This was built in 1908 for the Catalan Choral Society and is now the city's principal concert hall. It is a good example of Art Nouveau, decorated with statues and covered inside and out with brilliantly coloured mosaics. There is an inverted stained-glass cupola in the auditorium, stone roses bloom in profusion and stylised foliage grows up to the ceiling while galloping horses, Pegasus among them, approach from the opposite direction.

The nearby Grand Via, Barcelona's widest street and the shortest distance between the Costa del Maresme and the Costa Daurada, skirts past the Plaça de Toros Monumental, the larger of the two bullrings and by far the most obtrusive. It has a distinctly Moorish look with its blue and white tiles, slender arches and solid, comparatively plain towers, each supporting a large yellow, white and blue dome that could easily have come out of a box of gigantic, matching Easter eggs. There is also a comprehensive bullfighting museum, the Museu Taurino, that is usually crowded during the season.

On the far side of the Avinguda Diagonal, and only about four blocks away, is Antoni Gaudí's incredible Sagrada Familia which he intended to be a twentieth-century cathedral dedicated to the Holy Family. The building is not always seen in quite the same light; it has been called one of the wonders of the world, compared to the Taj Mahal and described as a work of genius. On the other hand, there are those who agree with George Orwell who thought it was hideous and blamed the anarchists for not blowing it up when they had the opportunity.

Gaudí took over the project from another architect in 1883 and eventually became so obsessed with it that he started living in a hut on the site, raising money from anyone he met and searching urgently for just the right people to use as models for all the different biblical characters he was planning to include. He did not expect the church to be finished in his lifetime but at the time of his death (he was killed by a tram in 1926) he had barely completed the Portal of the Nativity. This consists of three distinct sections: the Portal of Hope, showing the marriage of the Virgin, the Flight into Egypt and the Massacre of the Innocents; the Portal of Charity in the centre with Bethlehem as its main theme, surrounded by melting snow with a cypress tree on the top; and the Portal of Faith which concentrates on St Joseph and episodes from the boyhood of Christ.

Gaudí's original plans provided for twelve pinnacles symbolising the Apostles and four higher ones for the Evangelists, with those of Christ and the Virgin Mary towering over them. The various façades were to be in different symbolic colours, the main altar would have been plain and the interior, partly white and gold for rejoicing and partly in black and purple to signify mourning, lit by electronic beams. Following his death and burial in the crypt, which he had completed in 1887, work went on until the outbreak of the Civil War. After this, little was done until 1952 when the centenary of his birth resulted in a fresh burst of enthusiasm that upset some of his most ardent admirers. They argued that many of his plans and models were destroyed when part of the building (including his studio) was gutted, adding that Gaudí constantly changed his ideas as he went along and there was no-one left who knew him well enough to carry them through. Nobody knows if the Sagrada Familia will ever be completed but, for the moment at least, it remains one of the most tourist-conscious, emotive building sites in the country.

From the Sagrada Familia the Avinguda de Gaudí goes off at a tangent to the Hospital de Sant Pau, fronted by an exceptionally colourful section covered in mosaics and watched over by two angels. Other parts of the complex are surrounded with gardens and linked by underground passages but only a few areas, such as the stairway and the beautiful vaulted entrance, are open to the public. Beyond it is the Hospital de la Santa Creu, dating from the fifteenth century but added to at fairly regular intervals thereafter. It covers a large area, has some interesting features and is now occupied by a number of institutions as well as the Barcelona City Library.

Almost as widely publicised and as frequently visited as the Sagrada Familia is the Parc Güell on the Muntanya Pelada, easily accessible by car, taxi or underground train to Lesseps station, about 1km ($^1/_2$ mile) away. It is another unfinished Gaudí project, originally intended as a garden suburb and an example of modern town planning. However, due to the almost total lack of buildings, it has been turned into a fascinating park. There are only two houses of the sixty envisaged, one of which Gaudí had built for himself and lived in for about 20 years. It has now been turned into a museum, furnished in his own highly individual style and filled with memorabilia of various descriptions.

Parc l'Espanya Industrial

Gaudi's Casa Batlló with its iron balconies

The entrance to the park is flanked by two small gatehouses whose extraordinary roofs are patterned with ceramics, one of them with a curious, twisted spire. Two identical flights of steps join forces below the Hall of a Hundred Columns that would have been the local marketplace. The columns, there are actually only eighty-four of them, support a series of shallow domes covered in ceramic and glass mosaics. Stairs lead up to the flat roof, edged all round with a convoluted and deliberately uneven but brilliantly coloured stone seat which an audience could have used for concerts and other similar events. These days it gives sightseers an opportunity to take the weight off their feet while the centre makes a useful if rather dusty children's playground. The rest of the park is full of twisting roads and footpaths, arcades and viaducts. The church was never built but the site is marked by three stone crosses and has an excellent view over the city.

Barcelona is full of Gaudí's handiwork and that of his contemporaries, most of it a great deal closer to the Plaça de Catalunya. One of the most outstanding examples is the Casa Batlló, an apartment block on the Passieg de Gràcia with iron balconies shaped like masks, stained-glass windows and a roof tiled to resemble a dragon's scales supporting a group of rainbow-coloured chimneys. Further up, on the opposite side, is La Pedrera, also made up of apartments with a façade that overhangs the pavements in a series of wave-like balconies protected by intricate iron work. The terraced roof is an amazing mixture of spiral steps, giant crosses set with marble chips and chimneys that could easily have been inspired by a medieval knight. For anyone tired of Art Nouveau, the Museu de la Música, a block away on the Avinguda Diagonal, is Modernist in outlook but houses an interesting collection of antique and exotic musical instruments.

The Avinguda Diagonal continues to slice its way through the city, past the Plaça de Francesc Macià, where the Carrer de la Infanta Carlota branches off to the left towards the Parc l'Espanya Industrial, whose name does not really do it justice. The boating lake has been described as a modern version of the ancient Roman baths. There are stairways, sculptures, fountains and ornamental trees, lofty towers which look like lighthouses and a stylised dragon that makes an ideal children's slide. Nearby is the Plaça d'Espanya with its monumental fountain and reminders of the 1929 exhibition. To one side is the Plaça de Toros les Arenes, Barcelona's older, smaller and quieter bullring, while two large towers, said to have been inspired by the Campanile in Venice, guard the entrance to the Avinguda de la Reina

Maria Cristina. The buildings on either side of this wide thorough-fare are mostly exhibition halls. During the Fira de Mostres, in June, they help to turn it into the largest industrial marketplace in Spain. At the far end, beyond some mobile, illuminated fountains, a seemingly interminable flight of steps climbs up to the Palau Nacional which has been the home of the Museu d'Art de Catalunya for more than half a century. This is a vast neo-Classical building with domes and towers, balconies and balustrades. It looks impos-ing in the daylight and magnificent after dark, floodlit by an array of beams from hidden searchlights that radiate outwards like the spokes of a fan.

The museum itself has built up an outstandingly fine collection of medieval art. Frescoes of all descriptions were rescued from isolated little churches in the Pyrénées, including the twelfth-century *Sant Climent de Taüll*, generally regarded as the most exceptional of them all. There are also some memorable wood carvings such as the *Majestat Batlló* which portrays Christ on the cross in quite a different light. Instead of the usual agonised, half naked version, it shows a calm, well groomed figure wearing a brightly patterned tunic. Other notable exhibits include Lluís Dalmau's altarpiece *Verge del Consellers* in which a splendidly dressed Virgin, holding a naked Child, is plainly giving some thought to the advice of clergymen and various courtiers who are gathered round. Among several elegant examples of the work of Jaume Huguet is *Sant Jordi*, showing St George in a full suit of armour and a matching helmet complete with a jewelled band and his pennant flying from a flagpole on the top. More recent painters are also represented, including Ribera, Zurbarán, Velázques and El Greco, with a section devoted to the Catalan painter Antonio Viladomat.

The Museu d'Art de Catalunya shares part of the building with the Ceramics Museum which also has an interesting and varied collec- tion. Starting with some ancient pots from the Balearic Islands, it works its way forward through plates beautifully decorated with Moorish designs, medieval pottery, glazed tiles and eighteenth-century art work to many examples of contemporary ceramics. There are two more museums in the vicinity for people whose tastes lie in other directions. One is concerned with archaeology, delving back into prehistoric times when megaliths were all the rage. There are also Greek and Roman discoveries made in Empúries, on the Costa Brava, as well as vases, mosaics and other reminders of the early days of Barcelona. The Museu d'Etnologia is more cosmopoli- tan in its outlook, showing just as much enthusiasm for skeleton dolls from Mexico as it does for ritual paraphernalia from the Far East, artefacts from Africa and Latin America, shrunken heads, costumes and tools of all descriptions.

In sharp contrast to the Teatre Grec, fashioned out of an old stone quarry, surrounded by gardens and providing the open-air site for Barcelona's summer arts festival, is the nearby Fundació Miró. Located on Avinguda de Mirana, it is modern and angular, as befits a centre of contemporary art with paintings donated by Miró. Although popular, it has a more limited appeal than the Poble Espanyol, or Spanish Village, on the far side of the Palau Nacional. This is a collection of buildings designed to illustrate Spanish architecture through the ages and it was built for the exhibition of 1929. It is invariably crowded during opening hours when coachloads of tourists visit the Artes e Industrias Populares Museum devoted to local folklore and, in slightly fewer numbers, inspect the M·seu del Libro y de las Artes Graficas where the accent is on printing in its many different forms. Craftsmen can be seen at work, turning out high quality goods at predictably high prices and even the bars and restaurants cannot be accused of undercutting their competitors elsewhere.

Overlooking this whole area from the top of a rocky headland called Montjuïc, is an eighteenth-century fortress, Castell de Montjuïc, built in the form of a star with moats and pillboxes, which replaced the earlier Castell del Port. It is not exactly noted for its warlike achievements but earned a thoroughly unsavoury reputation as a prison up to and during the Civil War. In 1960 it was handed over to the city of Barcelona and transformed into a military museum (Museu Militar) with a nucleus of weapons collected by Frederic Marés. Nowadays it has a bit of everything, from scaled down versions of Catalan castles to model soldiers, battle plans and uniforms. The whole district takes its name from the headland, which some people say was originally the Mountain of Jupiter while others believe it is an abbreviation of the Mount of Jews, so-called because there was once a large Jewish cemetery there. It is possible to drive up, catch a bus, use one of the funiculars or opt for the cable car connecting the castle with a children's amusement park further down the hillside in the direction of the port.

Located about halfway between the castle and the Palau Nacional is what was once known as the Estadi Municipal de Montjuïc. However, it was the scene of feverish activity after 1986 when Barcelona was chosen as the venue for the summer Olympics of 1992, with the result that it has changed both its appearance and its name.

Although the city made three previous, unsuccessful attempts to host the Games — those of 1924, 1936 and 1972 — it can claim to have been associated with them for much longer than most of its rivals. In AD129 a citizen by the name of Lucius Minicius Natalis Quadronius Verus became an Olympic champion when he won the chariot race at the 227th Olympiad. The planners of what was hastily christened the Olympic Ring set about refurbishing the existing stadium behind its original façade and adding a sports palace for good measure. Additional sites also had to be found and those earmarked for development included the area round the Nou Camp football stadium (home to the Barcelona Football Club), the Vall d'Hebron and a length of beach now known as the Parc de Mar. Then there were hotels to build, roads to widen, airport facilities to update and extend in order to cope with a massive influx of visitors and a cleaning up operation to be organised and set in motion. It was a massive undertaking, and an extremely expensive one.

Anyone heading out of town along the Avinguda Diagonal will find plenty of interest in the area around the university campus, which was once the independent borough of Les Corts de Sarrià. The monastery of Pedralbes was founded in 1326 by Queen Elisenda de Montcada, who is buried in the church. The monastery still belongs to the order of Santa Clara and is a perfect example of Catalan medieval architecture — simple and understated with some fine stained glass, very viewable choir stalls, murals by Ferrer Bassá in the Capilla de Sant Miguel and a beautiful three-storey cloister which the nuns open to the public for a few hours every month.

By way of contrast, the Pedralbes Palace was built in the 1920s, designed and decorated in the Italian Renaissance style and used briefly by Alfonso XIII. It has now been turned into a museum, resplendent with tapestries, chandeliers, furniture and an assortment of objets d'art, in addition to which there is a carriage museum in the park. The original stables and porter's lodge on the Avinguda de Pedralbes were designed by Gaudí who provided them with a selection of his favourite archways and domes, liberally coated with ceramics, mosaics and tiles, and then added a splendidly ferocious wrought iron dragon to keep an eye on the entrance. It is now the headquarters of the Càtedra Gaudí, a department of the Polytechnical University of Catalunya and is used for the appropriate archives, a library and a small museum.

Tibidabo, the highest peak of the Collserola hills behind Barcelona, is worth visiting for its incomparable view, which may sometimes reach as far as Montserrat, the Pyrénées and even

Mallorca, and also because it can be great fun getting there. The Tramvia Blau, an archaic little blue tram which is a great favourite with citizens and visitors alike, sets off from the Avinguda de Tibidabo to make contact with a single-line funicular that climbs up the wooded hillside to the top. Once you are there, the attractions include a large neo-Gothic church, restaurants, bars and an amusement park with a huge ferris wheel and an entertaining mechanical doll museum (the Museu de Automatas de Tibidabo). Quite close by is the Observatori Fabra while, further west, a second funicular provides an alternative means of access to Vallvidrera, a residential area with Modernist overtones that is linked to both the summit and the city by attractive winding roads.

The Laberint d'Horta is worth visiting — the nineteenth-century mansion is surrounded by beautiful gardens containing, among other things, a secluded corner where cypress hedges have been trimmed to form a maze. Anyone who has the time and energy to explore on foot will come across old churches like the Santa María del Pi, modern sculptures, attractive fountains and intricately decorated buildings by the dozen. Two excellent examples are the Casa Macaya, at Passeig de Sant Joan 108, with its exceptionally fine courtyard and covered staircase, and the Casa de les Punxes, on the Avinguda Diagonal, whose round towers and spires shaped like witches' hats could have been left over from the Middle Ages. Even some of the street lights are highly individual and there are plenty of little shops tucked away out of sight that are worth the considerable effort it takes to find them.

It stands to reason that Barcelona, as the capital of Catalunya and an important seaport on the Mediterranean, has all the attributes of a sophisticated modern city. Nobody should have any difficulty in finding a suitable hotel, regardless of what they have in mind in the way of price, location, atmosphere and standards of comfort and service. There are some which are the last word in traditional luxury and at least half a dozen others in the first class bracket, many within easy shopping distance of the Avinguda Diagonal or the Barri Gòtic. Other very acceptable examples can be found throughout the city whose premises range from a converted palace or monastery to the purpose-built glass and concrete of the twentieth century. Lower down the price scale are hotels and *hostales* that can almost invariably be relied on to provide a lift and rooms en suite but may not have a restaurant or anywhere to park the car. Finally, there are a host of little places which can be charming or distinctly utilitarian, so it is as well to ask to see the room before arranging to move in. For young visitors on a tight budget there are one or two youth hostels with more still at the planning stage.

Restaurants, like hotels, are in good supply but vary a great deal. Some of the best and cheapest fish restaurants are to be found in Barceloneta, although there are also small, often atmospheric, places round the Barri Gòtic. During the high season these are nearly always inundated with tourists who tend to gravitate towards the Casa Culleretes in the Carrer Quintana, off the Carrer de Ferran. Founded in 1786, and said to be the oldest restaurant in Barcelona, it has changed very little down the years in either decor or popularity and serves some delicious traditional dishes.

At one time *escudella i carn d'olla* was an extremely popular local dish, eaten almost daily by the townspeople, but it seems to have gone out of fashion and seldom appears on any menu. It was a type of stew in which meat and vegetables were cooked together but served in two sections. The first course was a soup with rice and noodles followed by the remainder consisting of vegetables, black and white *butifarra*, a kind of sausage, and *pilota* which takes the form of meat balls blended with parsley, eggs and breadcrumbs. The unique taste comes from the extraordinary mixture of ingredients — everything from chicken, beef and pigs ears and trotters to marrow bones, cauliflower, cinnamon and garlic. This is usually followed by the Catalan version of crème caramel or a delicious soft white cheese. Another traditional delicacy which sometimes appears at breakfast is white bread spread with olive oil, salt and the flesh of a tomato, and there may also be ham or a thin omelette on top.

Many of the little bars serve *tapas* with their drinks. This is an idea borrowed from Andalucia and covers a multitude of totally unrelated items such as squid, shrimps, pieces of sausage, assorted vegetables, nuts and olives. They are set out on trays for customers to order and, as each portion arrives on a modest saucer, it is possible to sample a number of them and still look forward to dinner.

One of the most popular drinks is *cava*, the Spanish version of champagne, much of which comes from San Sadurni de Noya, 36km (22 miles) west of Barcelona. The two leading producers, Codorniu and Freixenet, are both happy to show visitors round their cellars and explain exactly how this sparkling wine is made. As the tours are conducted in four different languages — Catalan, Castilian, English and French — there is no need to take along a dictionary. Codorniu is the larger of the two and has its own Cava Museum, housed in a 100 year old building designed by one of Gaudí's contemporaries and full of wine-making equipment dating back to 1872.

In keeping with its cosmopolitan reputation, Barcelona stays up far into the night. The theatres and the opera and concert halls, along with similar places of entertainment, keep more or less conventional hours but many restaurants and bars stay open long after midnight. There are plenty of taxis and the metro operates from 5am to 11pm, with an extension to 1am on Saturdays, Sundays and holidays. Although most buses stop running at least an hour before midnight, one or two lines keep running until about 4.30am.

Barcelona is an ideal place to go shopping. There are three clearly defined areas for those in search of antiques, art galleries, jewellery, upmarket boutiques and expensive presents. Roughly speaking, the first is only a gentle stroll from the Plaça de Catalunya, filling the space between the Ramblas and the cathedral as far down as the Carrer de Ferran. The second lies in the opposite direction along the Rambla de Catalunya and the Passeig de Gràcia up to and slightly beyond the Avinguda Diagonal on the Via Augusta. The third is along the Diagonal itself, then up the Avinguda Pau Casals and around the Jardins d'Eduard Marquina. Each section has its department stores and shopping centres, whereas the Ramblas opt for souvenirs as well as international newspapers and flowers. The open-air markets, usually held once a week, can provide anything from basic requirements to colourful clothes.

Sports enthusiasts have just as much to keep them occupied. There are three golf courses within easy reach, the nearest being the Reial Club de Golf El Prat, a bare 15km (9 miles) away between the airport and the beach, with a long list of amenities including swimming pools and a children's nursery. The Club de Golf Sant Cugat is 20km (12 miles) distant, on the far side of the Collserola hills, reached along a minor road to Terrassa, the A7 motorway or by train at half-hourly intervals from the city centre. It is a hilly course, used as a military training ground during the Civil War but memorable chiefly as the place where Severiano Ballesteros made his debut as a professional. The Club de Golf Vallromanes, marginally further away, between El Masnou and Granollers, encourages young players as well as providing alternative attractions like a sauna, tennis and swimming along with the usual restaurant, sports shop and equipment for hire. For people who are not interested in golf there are riding stables, an ice rink, tennis and squash courts, a sailing school and plenty of swimming pools. Visitors who would rather spend their time sightseeing, but do not want to hire a car or make use of public transport, can join one of the many conducted tours. These may be confined to city attractions or take the form of longer excursions to places like

The Basilica of Montserrat monastery

Montserrat, the wine country or Tossa de Mar, or even a day out in Andorra up in the Pyrénées.

Long distance walkers or anyone with the stamina and enthusiasm to tackle a 50km (30 miles) hike into the mountains, would almost certainly find the GR6 very much to their liking. It starts off in the Vall d'Hebron and follows the old road through Valldaura to the top of the Collserola range before dropping down again through woodlands and past a couple of small hermitages to **Sant Cugat del Vallès**. In Roman times the town was known as *Castrum Octavianum* and had a little chapel housing the remains of Sant Cucufas who was murdered by Diocletian's forces in 303AD. Several centuries later it was replaced by a large abbey that survived until 1835, after which it was decided that some of the old buildings would do very nicely for a school. Although the church is not particularly memorable, the cloister is worth more than a passing glance. It is one of the biggest of its kind in Catalunya with 144 columns whose capitals were carved with biblical scenes, birds and acanthus leaves by one of the monks, Arnau Cadell. He even managed to include a working portrait of himself in the north-east corner and carved his name to make sure that he would be remembered.

The GR6 wanders on past the industrial city of **Terrassa** which was busy making fabrics in the Middle Ages and emphasises the fact in its Museu Textil. Some of the exhibits are very beautiful, especially the damasks and rich brocades as well as typically delicate materials from the Orient. The town was known as *Egara* to the Romans and became an important bishopric when the Visigoths took it over. Both sets of interlopers left their mark on a group of three historic churches on the hillside, not far from the castle-turned-monastery, now restored and used as a home for the municipal art museum. The churches are Sant Pere with its unusual tenth-century stone altar-piece; Sant Miguel, where the baptistry dome is supported by eight assorted columns with Roman and Visigoth handiwork, over a sarcophagus that serves as a font; and Santa María, complete with fourth-century mosaics and Gothic altarpieces by Jaume Huguet.

As far as English visitors are concerned, the most interesting murals are in the Santa María, recalling the murder of Thomas Becket, the ill-fated Archbishop of Canterbury, and painted shortly after his death in 1170. Beyond Terrassa the GR6 changes direction to call at Olesa de Montserrat, one of several places in Spain famous for its Passion Play, bypasses Collbató where there is a fascinating organ workshop, and joins the old road to what was once known as the Holy Mountain. The last part of the journey to the monastery of

Santa María de Montserrat is made in company with the GR5 that links Canet de Mar with Sitges.

Motorists bound for Montserrat will find almost as many, but very different, attractions if they decide to take a minor road along the Río Llobregat that marks the southern boundary of Barcelona. At **Torrelles de Llobregat**, for example, it is possible to obtain a Gulliver's eye view of many famous landmarks, scaled down to Lilliputian proportions and known as Catalunya en Miniatura.

Quite close by, on the road from Sant Boi de Llobregat to Sant Vicenç dels Horts, is the Colònia Güell. It is a small housing estate that owes its reputation to a crypt designed and built by Gaudí for the proposed church at Santa Coloma. It became a sort of testing ground for ideas that were used later in the construction of the Sagrada Familia. The little hooded windows, with their attractive wrought iron grilles, look out on pine woods while a wide stone stairway leads up to the roof where the church was to have been built. The crypt itself is dark with a vaulted roof, supported by slanted columns of rough-cut stone, designed in five sections and held together with lead. The stained glass in the windows radiates out like the petals of a flower while the pews, also designed by Gaudí and made of polished wood and iron, would not look out of place as desks in some exclusive schoolroom.

Beyond Sant Vicenç dels Horts the N11 follows the river to Abrera where there is a right-hand fork to **Montserrat**. The road up to the monastery is wide and well graded but the volume of traffic heading in each direction makes it rather difficult for drivers to admire the scenery. Eventually the monastery comes into view, surrounded on all sides by extraordinary rock formations. Some of them are serrated or worn into pinnacles, which have led a number of observers to describe it as the 'saw-toothed mountain', while others are smooth and rounded with enormous circular boulders on top that make them look like gigantic figures silhouetted against the sky.

This weird, and certainly unusual massive outcrop has been regarded as a holy place for about 2,000 years, attracting hermits in search of solitude and giving rise to the inevitable crop of legends. One of them maintains that a figure of the Virgin, carved in an inspired moment by St Luke, was hidden by St Peter in a convenient cave. Another insists that the Holy Grail was discovered in the vicinity by Sir Parsifal, thereby inspiring Wagner to compose his opera of the same name and give it a comparable setting.

The Virgin was allegedly found by shepherds towards the end of the ninth century and, when she could not be moved from the mountain, a chapel was built on the spot. Shortly afterwards, a group of monks from Ripoll moved in and laid the foundations for a monastery which became increasingly rich and powerful as well as a place of pilgrimage second only to Santiago de Compostela. During the Peninsular War the Catalan guerrillas had no compunction about turning it into a fortress which led to its destruction by the French in 1811. Later the whole complex was restored and, to a certain extent, building has been going on ever since. It now has hotels and self-service restaurants, a youth hostel and a campsite, souvenir shops, two cable cars and two funiculars. About 30 years ago groups of monks and choristers could be seen wandering round the courtyards but their place has been taken by day trippers, backpackers and other tourists, with only an occasional pilgrim. However, the faithful still turn up in droves for the special services on 27 April and 8 September.

The most impressive building is undoubtedly the basilica, although this suffered at the hands of the French and only part of the cloister, built by Philip II, managed to escape. The famous Black Mare de Déu de Montserrat, now encased in glass for safety's sake, has her own allotted space behind the high altar. The church is crammed with gifts that flooded in to replace its vanished treasures but none of them is at all remarkable, a criticism which can also be levelled at most of the pictures and archaeological exhibits on display. A footpath leads up to the Santa Cova, where the statue of the Virgin is supposed to have been discovered, while another makes for the Sant Miguel hermitage and then presses on to the Sant Jeroni belvedere. This has a panoramic view of the Pyrénées and the Balearic Islands, but only when the weather is clear.

Still further inland from Montserrat, the town of **Manresa** is justly proud of its collegiate church of Santa María, known inaccurately as La Seu because it has never been given the status of a cathedral. It dates largely from the fourteenth century and has quite an impressive collection of sacred art. Anyone who is interested in ancient castles that have been turned into *paradores* might consider driving on to **Cardona**, a pleasant town in the Cardener valley whose nearest neighbour is a mountain consisting entirely of salt. The castle-cum-*parador* and the former monastery of Sant Vicenç are perched on a hilltop outside the town which also has a delightful old parish church, several medieval mansions and an antiquated bridge, started in the fifteenth century but unfinished.

Just outside Manresa, a secondary road makes tracks for Vic with an optional side trip to **L'Estany**, a twelfth-century village whose church was damaged in the earthquake of 1428. However, it has managed to preserve some unusual art work, including griffons, wedding scenes and musicians, very like the ceramics made in Paterna, outside Valencia, in the thirteenth century.

Vic, an industrial centre in the foothills of the Pyrénées, is a cathedral city occupying the site of an old Iberian town of which nothing tangible remains. However, there are a few remnants from a Roman temple and an extremely comprehensive Museu Episcopal. Among its most noteworthy exhibits are part of the Erill-la-Vall *Descent from the Cross*, a fresco of the Last Supper and an alabaster altarfront of the Life of Christ, carved in 1341. Much of the old Romanesque cathedral was knocked down about 200 years ago to make way for a more up-to-date model but fortunately a number of things were preserved such as the altarpiece and a massive grille that was transferred into all that remained of the original cloister. There are some old houses facing the Plaça del Mercadal, where weekly markets have been held for about 1,000 years, and an old bridge or two, the most viewable of which is the Pont d'en Bruguer. Vic has its own *parador*, a modern version of a typical country house overlooking a man-made lake, as well as a couple of quite well equipped hotels, a sprinkling of Art Nouveau and an excellent road to Barcelona, just over 60km (37 miles) away.

Additional Information

Places of Interest

Barcelona
Archaeological Museum
Parc de Montjuïc
Open: 9.30am-1.30pm and 4-7pm
Tuesday to Saturday. 9.30am-2pm
Sunday and holidays. Closed
Monday. ☎ 423 21 49 or 423 56 01

Casa Batlló
Passeig de Gràcia
Visits arranged on request.
☎ 204 52 50

Cathedral Museum
Plaça de la Seu

Open: daily 11am-1pm.
☎ 315 35 55

Codorniu Wine Cellars
San Sadurni de Noya
Cellars and Cava Museum
Open: 9am-11am and 3-5pm
Monday to Thursday. Morning
only on Friday. Closed Saturday,
Sunday, holidays, Easter week,
during August and 25 and 26
December.
☎ 93 891 0125

Colónia Güell
☎ 93 661 29 36 for details of visiting
hours.

Freixenet Wine Cellars
San Sadurni de Noya
Open: 9am-12noon and 3.30-6pm
Monday to Friday. Saturday
morning by appointment. Closed
Saturday, Sunday and holidays.
☎ 93 891 0700 for details of tours
during the last week of December.

Fundació Joan Miró
Parc de Montjuïc
Open: 11am-7pm Tuesday to
Saturday. 10am-2.30pm Sunday
and holidays. Closed Monday.
☎ 329 19 08

Gran Teatre de Liceu
Rambla dels Caputxins
Tours 11.30am and 12.15pm
Monday and Friday.

La Pedrera
Passeig de Gràcia
Patio and terrace open: 10am,
11am, 12noon, 2pm and 6pm on
weekdays and 10am, 11am and
12noon Saturday.

Les Drassanes (Museu de Maritim)
Portal de la Pau
Open: 10am-2pm and 4-7pm
Tuesday to Saturday. 10am-2pm
Sunday and holidays. Closed
Monday. ☎ 318 32 45 or 301 64 25

Museu d'Art de Catalunya
Palau Nacional
Open: 9am-2pm Tuesday to
Sunday. Closed Monday.
☎ 423 18 24

Museu Etnológico
Parc de Montjuïc
Open: 9am-8.30pm Tuesday to
Saturday. 9am-2pm Sunday and
holidays. Closed Monday.
☎ 424 64 02 or 424 68 07

Museu d'Historia de la Ciutat
Plaça del Rei
Open: 9am-8.30pm Tuesday to
Saturday. 9am-1.30pm Sunday and
holidays. Closed Monday.
☎ 315 11 11

Museu de Autómatas del Tibidabo
Open: 11am-8pm April to September and 11am-8pm on Saturday,
Sunday and holidays October to
March. ☎ 211 79 42

Museu de Cera
Rambla de Santa Monica
Open: 11am-1.30pm and 4.30-
7.30pm Monday to Friday.
☎ 317 26 49

Museu del Fútbol Club Barcelona
At the Nou Camp stadium
Open: 10am-1pm Monday to
Saturday and 4-7pm on holidays
from April to September. 10am-
1pm Tuesday to Friday and 4-6pm
Saturday, Sunday and holidays
October to March. Closed Monday
from October to March but
otherwise on Sunday. ☎ 330 94 11

Museu de la Música
Av. Diagonal 373
Open: 9am-2pm Tuesday to Sunday. Closed Monday. ☎ 217 11 57

Museu del Perfume
Plaça de Gràcia
Open: 10am-1.30pm and 4-7.30pm
Monday to Friday. Closed
Saturday, Sunday and holidays.
☎ 215 72 38

Museu de Zoología
Parc de la Ciutadella
Open: 9am-2pm Tuesday to
Sunday. Closed Monday.
☎ 319 69 50 or 319 69 12

Museu Marés
Plaça Sant Iu
Open: 9am-2pm and 4-7pm
Tuesday to Saturday. 9am-2pm
Sunday and holidays. Closed
Monday.
☎ 310 58 00

Museu Militar
Castell de Montjuïc
Open: 10am-2pm and 4-7pm
Tuesday to Saturday. 10am-7pm
Sunday and holiday. Closed
Monday.
☎ 329 86 13

Museu Picasso
Montcada 15/19
Open: 10am-7.30pm. Closed
Mondays.
☎ 319 63 10 or 315 47 61

Museu Taurino
In the bullring on the Grand Via
Open: daily 10am-1pm and 3.30-
7pm during the season from April
to September.
☎ 245 58 03 or 232 71 58

Museum of Modern Art
Parc de la Ciutadella
Placa d'Armes
Open: 9am-7.30pm Tuesday to
Saturday. 9am-2pm Sunday and
holidays. 3am-7.30pm Monday.
☎ 319 57 28 or 310 63 08

Palau Güell
Carrer Nou de la Rambla
Theatre Museum open: 10am-1pm
and 5-6pm. Sunday 10am-1pm.
☎ 317 39 74

Palau de la Generalitat
Plaça de Sant Jaume
Open: 10am-2pm Sunday.

Palau de la Virreina
Rambla de les Flors
Open: 9.30am-2pm and 6-9pm
Tuesday to Saturday. Closed
Sunday, Monday and holidays.
☎ 302 14 30

Parc Güell
Casa-Museu Gaudí
Open: daily 10am-2pm and 4-7pm
March to November. Closed
December to February.
☎ 214 64 46 or 317 52 21

Pedralbes
Monastery Museum
Open: 9.30am-2pm. Closed
Monday and holidays.
☎ 203 92 82 or 204 27 47

Palau Reial de Pedralbes
Av. Diagonal
Open: 10am-1pm and 4-6pm
Tuesday to Friday. 10am-1.30pm
Saturday, Sunday and holidays.
Closed Monday.
☎ 203 75 00 or 204 63 19

Poble Espanyol
☎ 423 01 96 for the museums, also
426 19 99

Sagrada Familia
Studio in the crypt
Open: daily 9am-9pm July and
August. 9am-8pm April to June.
9am-7pm September to March.
☎ 255 02 47

Montserrat
The famous boys choir, founded in
thirteenth century, can be heard at
1pm and 6.45pm except in July.

Museu de Montserrat
Open: 10am-1.30pm and 4-7pm
Tuesday to Saturday.

Tourist Offices

Arenys de Mar
Rambla Bisbe Pol 8
Open: 1 June to 30 September.
☎ 93 792 02 42

Barcelona
Plaça Sant Jaume
In the City Hall
Open: 9am-9pm Monday to Friday.
9am-3pm Saturday.
☎ 301 74 43

Central Station-Sants
Open: daily 8am-8pm.
☎ 410 25 94

Moll de la Fusta
In the port area
Open: daily 8am-8pm.
☎ 317 30 41

Plaça Univers
Open: 10am-2pm and 4-8pm, but
only when the fair is open.
☎ 325 52 35

Poble Espanyol (Spanish Village)
Open: 10am-2pm and 3-7pm.

Gran Via Corts Catalanes 658
Open: 9am-9pm Monday to Friday.
9am-3pm Saturday.
☎ 301 74 43

Airport
Open: 9.30am-8pm Monday to
Friday. 9.30am-3pm Saturday.
☎ 325 58 29

Canet de Mar
Carretera Nacional II
Open: 15 June to 15 September.
☎ 93 794 08 98

Cardona
Plaça de la Fira 1
☎ 93 869 10 00

Manresa
Plaça Major
☎ 93 872 53 78

Mataró
Carrer de la Riera 48
☎ 93 796 01 80

Sant Cugat del Vallès
Plaça de Barcelona 17
☎ 93 674 09 50

Vic
Plaça Major
☎ 93 886 20 91

3

COSTA DAURADA

If the name Costa Daurada, or Dorada, sounds more familiar than the Costa del Maresme, it may be because of the number of people who have spent a holiday in Sitges or received postcards from this popular seaside resort. However, visitors looking for the best of both worlds — sightseeing in Barcelona combined with a beautiful sandy beach on the doorstep — would probably find **Castelldefels** more convenient. It has the advantage of being only 24km (15 miles) from Barcelona along a fast dual carriageway and can offer a variety of hotels, some with their own tennis courts and swimming pools. It becomes rather crowded during the season, especially as there is also a campsite quite close by, but it is possible to get away from it all and explore the cliffs, creeks and coves of the Garraf massif slightly to the south.

An added attraction is the Celler Güell in **Garraf**, a small fishing village that is rapidly becoming a tourist resort. The Celler is an oddly shaped stone building designed by Gaudí that seems unable to decide which century it represents. The main section is triangular with sloping sides and futuristic chimneys whereas the adjoining wall and the round tower behind hark back to the Middle Ages.

Sitges, with its crescents of golden sand, is somewhat larger but manages to combine a nucleus of narrow winding streets and attractive whitewashed houses with highrise holiday accommodation and the obligatory campsites, bars, restaurants and discos. In the past it was kept busy loading and unloading the *barcas de mitjana*, typical Catalan vessels that were used for trading along the Mediterranean coast. However, at the turn of the century the town was adopted by the luminist school of painters after Santiago Rusiñol converted a group of fishermen's cottages into the present Cau Ferrat

Museum which takes its name from his large collection of wrought iron. As Sitges castle had recently been demolished he was able to rescue a number of useful items from the site. This resulted in an elegant mansion which is now filled with paintings, sculptures and ceramics, as well as some very worthwhile furniture.

Much the same tactics were employed to turn the fourteenth-century Hospital de Sant Joan next door into the Museu Maricel. Here, among other things, a staircase from Solivella castle vies for attention with both medieval and modern works of art. Two interesting examples are an alabaster figure of the Virgin from Sant Miguel de Fai and Josep Sert's mural inspired by World War I. By way of a change, the Casa Llopis Museum, on the Carrer Sant Josep, takes a lighthearted look at life in the eighteenth and nineteenth centuries, concentrating on popular pastimes, mechanical gadgets, musical boxes and a splendidly varied collection of dolls. Finally, the Vinyet Hermitage, unexpectedly ornate and full of ex voto offerings, has a model ship under full sail suspended from the roof.

Sitges has its full quota of Modernist architecture, several monuments to artists like El Greco and Rustinöl and the Terramar garden suburb, said to be one of the first of its kind in Europe. The Club de Golf Terramar is conveniently sited at the end of the promenade overlooking the sea. It not only has a dovecote, a water hazard, trees and palms but also tennis courts, swimming pools, a children's nursery and a restaurant as well as carts and clubs for hire. The Aiguadolç pleasure boat harbour, within easy reach of the town, keeps well over 100 berths for visitors and provides shops, restaurants, a disco and organised entertainments. Sitges celebrates in style. There is an antique car rally during Carnival, the streets are carpeted with flowers for Corpus Christi and carnations, the national flower of Spain, have their own individual show in May. The rest of the year is taken up with events such as concerts, theatre festivals and the Cine Fantástico y de Terror at the end of October.

From Sitges a secondary road heads inland to Sant Pere de Ribes, less well known for its church and castle than for the Gran Casino de Barcelona, elegantly housed in the Palau del Solers. A little further on, **Vilafranca del Penedés** has been an important wine producing centre for a long time, judging by the enormous sixteenth-century press standing alongside the road to Tarragona. Its Museu del Vi is part of the fourteenth-century palace of the kings of Aragon, a church and other elderly buildings surrounding the Plaça Jaume I. A good deal of space is devoted to the history of wine, starting with the Egyptians and the Romans and working up to the nineteenth century with the help of an assortment of bottles and antiquated pieces of equipment. Some of the cellars are open to the public. Other sections content themselves with displays of art and archaeology, especially discoveries made at the ruins of Olèrdola, an ancient walled settlement with Iberian and Roman connections.

Vilanova i la Geltrú, a few kilometres down the coast from Sitges, has fewer tourists but just as many local visitors, a pleasant beach, facilities for water sports, a harbour for fishing boats and pleasure craft, and several interesting museums. One of the most fascinating is the Casa Papiol, the home of a wealthy landowner at the beginning of the nineteenth century which has been preserved down to the smallest detail. There are luxurious apartments decorated in a variety of styles, a billiard room, kitchens, stables and a private chapel with a shrine containing the relics of an early Roman martyr.

The Balaguer Museum has everything from an Egyptian mummy with its burial accoutrements, examples of Oriental art, weapons and coins to comparatively modern paintings. These include an *Annunciation* by El Greco with a heavenly orchestra providing a musical accompaniment on a variety of instruments, among them a cello resting improbably on a cloud. The Castillo de la Geltrú, more of a mansion than a castle, divides its attention between medieval exhibits, seventeenth-century ceramics and modern art. In addition there is a Railway Museum, the Casa de Santa Teresa (full of furniture and pictures) and the Roig Toques Maritime Museum that concerns itself mainly with navigation.

Coma-ruga is blessed with magnificent beaches that fully justify the title of Costa Daurada, or Golden Coast. So far it is blissfully free of highrise buildings and the trappings of tourism, although the sands continue in an almost unbroken line down past Torredembarra, with its ruined castle, to Altafulla, where the shoreline is edged with trees. **El Vendrell**, slightly inland from Coma-ruga, was the birthplace of Pau Casals, the great Catalan cellist and composer who was born in a house on the Carrer Santa Anna in 1876. He refused to live in Spain under the Franco regime, spent several years at Conflent in France and died in Puerto Rico in 1973. His holiday home overlooking the sea at Sant Salvador has been turned into a museum containing many of his most cherished possessions and concerts are held quite frequently in the auditorium that was built next door. In 1979 his remains were brought back to Spain and buried in the cemetery at El Vendrell.

Anyone in search of history, atmosphere and ancient buildings in an excellent state of preservation need look no further than

Tarragona. It is also very much in tune with modern times, having a thriving petrochemical industry and an extremely busy dock area, said to handle a greater volume of goods than any other port in Spain. In addition, it is a most attractive city, rising up in tiers from the waterfront with wide avenues and some interesting modern architecture in the Eixample, a comparatively new district designed in 1922. Although not nearly so extensive as its counterpart in Barcelona, it was laid out along very similar lines and is extremely proud of its covered market on the Plaça de Corsini and several other buildings like the Casa Salas on the Rambla Nova.

There is little doubt that Tarragona's chief attraction is its ancient city which, according to one school of thought, was founded in about 1000BC on a hill overlooking the Mediterranean and only appropriated later by the Iberians. The Romans took an instant liking to it when they set out from Empúries to extend their influence over a wide area of the peninsula. They settled in, renamed it *Tarraco* and provided it with a whole province of its own. Eventually, this one-time settlement developed into the largest, most elegant and most important city on the coast. It was seven times the size of *Barcino*, now known as Barcelona, and praised by men like Pliny for its perfect

Relaxing in the sun at Coma-ruga

climate and delicious wines. Almost immediately, the Romans started building an artificial harbour protected by breakwaters whose pylons and connecting arches survived for several hundred years. Unfortunately, the base of the only remaining pylon was blown up in 1843 when improvements were being made to cope with an increasing trade in wines, cereals and dried fruit. The Romans were followed by the Visigoths and later by the Moors, who were finally driven out by Ramón Berenguer. There followed another, less impressive spell in the limelight before Tarragona went into a decline during the fifteenth century and rested on its ancient laurels for the next 300 years.

The original city, on its fairly substantial hill, is surrounded by massive walls, built by the Romans on the foundations laid down for earlier, equally impressive ramparts. These were regularly maintained and updated until the eighteenth century when the English added an outer perimeter during the Spanish War of Succession in an attempt to keep the French at bay. Just outside the walls, overlooking the sea, are the remains of the Roman amphitheatre where Bishop Fructuosus and two of his clergy were martyred in AD259. Traces of a church built on the spot where they were burned to death have been discovered in the ruins of Santa Maria del Miracle which replaced it about 800 years ago.

A short walk away, inside the ramparts, on the Passeig de Sant Antoni, is the Praetorium. It dates from the first century BC and was lived in at various times by both Augustus and Hadrian. Pontius Pilate is said to have been born here. No very drastic changes were made to the building until it was converted into a royal palace in the fourteenth century and provided with a large Gothic extension that acts as an annex for the Museu Arqueològic next door. All the exhibits in the archaeological museum were discovered in and around the city. They include remnants from the temples of Jupiter and Augustus, statues that once adorned the ancient squares and public buildings, and some interesting mosaics. Among these, pride of place goes to the Head of Medusa with her wide, staring eyes, a distinct pout and a healthy crop of snakes. The area bordering on the museum was originally the Jewish quarter where the Plazuela Angels marks the site of their old synagogue. The fourteenth-century Carrer Merceria, with its Gothic arcades, makes a bee-line for the equally atmospheric Carrer Major, joining forces at the foot of a flight of steps leading up to the cathedral from the Plaça de la Seu. It is almost impossible to get an overall view of this remarkably imposing church because of the straightjacket of antiquated buildings hemming it in on every side. Some of them are worth inspecting in their own right, such as the Cambreria, partly enclosing the Plaça de la Seu; the former Hospital de Santa Tecla which started life on the Avinguda dels Coques in the eleventh century and the Casa del Degà with its embedded tombstones, two of which have inscriptions in Hebrew.

The cathedral was built on the site of a large temple to Jupiter and incorporates part of the original walls. The main façade is memorable chiefly for its superb rose window, a statue of the Virgin and the sculptured figures of the apostles by Master Bartomeu standing in their decorative niches rather more than head high on either side of the entrance. The interior is dark but in no way dismal, with just enough light to make out the intricate carving on the altarpiece, the tomb of archbishop Juan of Aragon, the Capella dels Sastres and a second beautifully proportioned doorway leading to the cloister. The Museu Diocesano in the chapter house has its own assortment of treasures including a statue of the Mare de Déu del Claustre and a sizeable collection of tapestries, one of them depicting 'The Good Life', or La Bon Vida, of the fifteenth century.

A short walk away, near the Rosary Gate, are the somewhat sparse remains of the large Roman Forum but they prove to be less interesting than the Necrópolis and Paleo-Christian Museum on the Avinguda Ramón y Cajal, almost on the river bank. This was apparently a pagan burial ground before the early Christians started using it for their own tombs in the third century and kept up the practice for the next 300 years. A number of sarcophagi are strategically arranged under the trees while others are housed in a museum in the gardens alongside other discoveries from the site. Among the most interesting are the so-called lion sarcophagus and a small ivory doll, along with the two-handled jugs used by the Greeks and Romans to hold liquids, other utensils and some mosaics. Next door is an important looking building behind tall, well guarded iron gates which could easily be taken for a senior government administrative centre but is actually the local tobacco factory. Other places of interest are the Museu d'Historia de Tarragona and the much publicised Passeig Arquelògic along a section of the ramparts. A nearby path through exceedingly well-kept gardens has an uninterrupted view of the walls as the Bourbons must have seen them when they marched on Tarragona at the beginning of the eighteenth century.

Roughly 4km ($2^1/_2$ miles) from the city, standing back from the road to Valls, is a large, honeycoloured Roman viaduct sometimes referred to as the Devil's Bridge. It can either be admired from a distance or inspected at close quarters after a pleasant stroll through the surrounding pine woods. Slightly further afield, in the direction of Reus, is the Centcellas Mausoleum, standing among the vineyards near the village of Constanti. It is another Roman relic, this time attributed to a wealthy landowner with Christian sympathies. The mausoleum consists of two large chambers, one of which has a vast cupola decorated with some graphic mosaics combining biblical stories with typical hunting scenes.

Modern Tarragona regards the two parallel Ramblas — Vella and Nova — as its most important thoroughfares. They are within easy walking distance of the old city and share the Passeig de les Palmeres which looks out across the port, the long sandy Playa del Milagro and

Locals forming a tower of men, Tarragona

The Arco de Bará, Tarragona

Cambrills is a budding tourist resort
with moorings for pleasure craft and a long sandy beach

the Roman amphitheatre to the open sea. Each of them can provide hotel accommodation as well as shops and restaurants. There is a choice of eight local campsites. The Tarragona Sailing Club, the first to be established in Catalunya and one of the oldest in Spain, has its premises at the far end of the harbour beyond the fishing fleet and reserves a limited number of berths for visitors.

Ramblers can opt for either the GR92 that explores the coastal area on both sides of the city or follow the GR72 up into the mountains. It links Constanti and Reus with the GR7, stops to inspect the Santes Creus monastery, climbs up almost to the summit of Montagut and pauses at the delightful town of La Llacuna before heading for Montserrat. The Club de Golf Costa Daurada is 5km (3 miles) from Tarragona on the road to El Catllar, off either the N340 or the motorway. Although it only has nine holes, there are water hazards, large bunkers and plenty of trees in the grounds of a country house which also provides facilities for tennis, swimming and squash.

Tarragona has a magnificent beach of its own but holidaymakers with only a minimal interest in antiquities usually make for **Salou**, a highrise tourist resort about 10km (6 miles) further down the coast. Most of the buildings are apartment blocks, providing accommodation that only just manages to cope at the height of the season when the normal population of about 20,000 increases substantially. It is probably just as well that a large percentage of holidaymakers settle down happily on one of the dozen or more different campsites, especially those with bungalows to rent. Apart from all the ingredients of any thriving coastal resort, such as golden sands, blue seas, organised entertainments and a sweeping promenade, there are some enticing little coves and inlets to explore on Cap Salou nearby.

It may not be very long before Salou is linked with **Cambrils**, a fraction further round the bay, which describes itself as a fishing port but has every intention of joining the lucrative tourist scene. It has got off to a good start with a colourful fish market, moorings for pleasure craft, a clutch of quite well equipped hotels and some of the best fish restaurants to be found anywhere along the coast. It also provides plenty of campsites, some with bungalows, a number of which stay open right through the year. Cambrils is the ideal place to sample a whole range of traditional dishes including *arroz abanda* which, incidentally, should only be ordered in a reputable restaurant. It consists of rice, boiled with a good many different types of fish and seafood such as lobsters, prawns and squids, congers, groupers and angler fish. The rice is served first, but this is optional, followed by the fish in a sauce called *romesco* which may be simply olive oil, bread and a special variety of red peppers. It can also be given a new dimension by adding garlic, almonds, cognac and vinegar. There is not much to see in the town itself but a minor road takes a somewhat roundabout route to the castle-convent of Sant Miguel d'Escornalbou, near the village of Riudecanyes. Apart from some impressive ruins, with a view to match, Escornalbou castle makes a feature of its large library and admirable collections of furniture and ceramics.

Another minor road cuts across country from Riudecanyes to **Reus**, the main town in the area, which has an airport, one or two small hotels and three fairly interesting museums. The Comarcal is mainly concerned with local history, painting, sculpture and ceramics, leaving the Salvador Villas a free hand with archaeology and the Rull Museum to devote itself to pictures. Apart from markets, fairs and exhibitions, the other local attractions include some very decorative Modernist buildings such as the Institue Pere Mata where Lluis Domènech i Montaner tried out some of the ideas he was to develop later for the Hospital de Sant Pau in Barcelona. The Casa Navàs, on the Plaça del Mercadal, is just as eye-catching, with glazed tiles, stained glass, leather furniture and sculptures by an artist called Gaudí who was a cousin of the famous architect.

Several options are open to the motorist who wants to explore the mountains north of Reus and does not mind negotiating the incredibly twisty little roads, parts of which demand careful attention. However, they do not usually carry a lot of traffic so there are no real problems if you drive carefully. Among the places worth visiting are Siurana de Prades, with an Arab castle where the Moors held out until 1153, and **Prades** itself. It is a charming little village that owes its nickname of Vila Vermella to the reddish coloured stone that was used for several of its ancient buildings. Apart from the remaining walls and two arched gateways, there is an unusual fountain in the arcaded Plaça Major, fed by an underground spring which the local inhabitants say has never run dry.

Alternatively, a fairly straight but generally less attractive secondary road connects Reus with **Montblanc**, one of the most carefully preserved fortified medieval towns in Catalunya. The extensive walls, with their evenly spaced towers, were built towards the end of the fourteenth century, enclosing a typical city of the time with characteristic mansions and an interesting selection of churches to match. The oldest of these is Sant Miguel but it is not as decorative as the larger church of Santa María. This was partly constructed by an Englishman, Reinald Fonoll, and took nearly 200 years to build —

even then it was not completely finished. Its prize possessions are a fourteenth-century stone altarpiece and a Gothic statue of the Virgin, whereas the former Hospital de Sant Marçal was presented with a number of appropriate items by Frederic Marès.

Montblanc's other attractions include a Gothic bridge over the Río Francolí near the Hospital de Santa Magdalena, which has a most attractive cloister, the Convent de la Mercè and the shrine of La Serra whose Virgin is the patron saint of the town. Also outside the walls are the sadly neglected remains of the Convent de Sant Francesc whose fourteenth-century church was used as a warehouse until it was rescued and restored in 1987. At about the same time as the church was built, a young friar called Anselm Turmeda turned his back on the monastery, moved to Tunis and became a Muslim. He earned an enviable reputation as a writer under his new name of abd'Allah al-Turguman and his books were widely read in Catalunya. Although the Church was willing to forgive him, he refused to return to Spain and died in Tunis in 1425.

Mainly because the fortified gateways were too narrow to cope with the ever increasing amount of traffic, the N240 from Tarragona to Lleida bypasses the old town. However, anyone in search of a bed and bath for the night can choose between a fairly modest local hotel with a restaurant and space to park the car, and a smaller but more upmarket establishment on the main road about 8km (5 miles) away.

One place in the area that should definitely not be missed is the monastery of Santa María de Poblet, near L'Espluga de Francolí. It is a magnificent religious complex founded in 1151 when Ramón Berenguer made a small piece of the countryside available to the abbey of Fontfreda, near Narbonne, for a new Cistercian monastery. The chosen spot was a remote but fertile valley surrounded by forests which were responsible for the name Poblet, derived from the Latin *populetum*, meaning a grove of white poplars. The project started off in quite a small way, beginning with a church, the refectory, St Stephen's cloister and an infirmary. However, agriculture was one of the Cistercians' strong points and within 50 years the monastery had accumulated enough land for seventeen different farms, most of them in western Catalunya. Gradually the emphasis on austerity and service gave way to avarice and political wheeling and dealing until, in its heyday, Poblet owned sixty villages, appointed the mayors of ten separate towns and had jurisdiction over seven baronies.

This heady combination of wealth, power and royal patronage led to an extensive building programme which included a palace and

The church of Santa María in Montblanc

ramparts 608m (2,000ft) long, 11m (36ft) high and 2m (6½ft) thick, complete with battlements and more than a dozen towers. A much less attractive manifestation was a total disregard for the welfare of everyone else in the region. As a result, when measures were introduced in 1835 to suppress the various religious orders and confiscate their property, the Catalan population went to work with a will. Poblet was overrun, its buildings damaged, its treasures looted or destroyed and its famous library of books and manuscripts burned. The ruins were left to moulder until 1930 when a board of trustees was set up to organise a reconstruction programme and 10 years later four Italian monks were installed as the nucleus of the present Poblet brotherhood. The outcome exceeded all expectations, recreating much of its past splendour while at the same time reintroducing the true spirit of the Cistercian order.

A tour of the monastery includes the twelfth-century church with its enormous carved altarpiece and suspended crucifix but very little additional decoration. On either side of the nave are the tombs of the kings of Aragon; Jaume I, Pedro III and his three wives and Ferdinand I to the north and Alfonso I, Joan I, with two wives, and Joan II, who only had one, lying opposite them. Alfonso IV and Martin I are buried elsewhere in the church. The royal remains had to be removed to Tarragona cathedral in 1843 for safekeeping but they were returned about 100 years later when Frederic Marès was given the job of repairing all the damage that had been done to their alabaster tombs. The cloister is especially memorable and so is the chapter house with the tombstones of twelve early abbots laid out in a line level with the floor. Beyond it is the library and above them both the spacious thirteenth-century dormitory where massive central arches support the wooden beams of the roof. The section reserved for retired monks has been turned into a museum and so have the royal apartments, displaying some original sculptures, a comprehensive collection of wooden statues, gold and silverware and other artefacts as well as documents relating to the reconstruction work carried out over the past 50 years. Also worth seeing are the two entrances, known respectively as the Golden Door and the Royal Door, the kitchen and refectory and the enormous vaulted wine cellar that could easily pass for a church.

Driving back to Tarragona along the N240, the first place of interest is **Valls**, a largely commercial centre with very little to show from its medieval past except for an old archway leading to the Jewish quarter. The church of Sant Joan Baptista is fairly nondescript although the Chapel des Roser has a scene from the Battle of Lepanto on a number of glazed tiles added in the seventeenth century. The town is famous for building *castellers*, a tradition that has an enthusiastic following all over Catalunya. The idea is to create a tower of men standing on each others shoulders, usually with three at each level, growing younger and lighter as it gets nearer to the top. Meanwhile, the rest of the town crowds round, providing encouragement and additional support. The Xiquets de Valls team reached such a peak of perfection that a special monument showing them in action stands at a busy intersection near the main road. Another time-honoured custom is the *calcotada*, when freshly picked shallots are roasted over an open fire and eaten with a special sauce whose ingredients are a closely guarded secret. This has developed into a popular tourist attraction, especially as the shallots are often followed by grilled cutlets and plenty of local wine.

From Valls there is one excellent reason for turning off the main route to Tarragona and taking the C246, followed by a smart turn off to **Aiguamúrcia**. It is only a small village with some unremarkable modern buildings, but the famous Santes Creus monastery is very close at hand. Santes Creus and Poblet have a lot in common but they also differ in a great many respects. They both belonged to the Cistercians, were founded in the twelfth century, patronised by royalty and systematically enlarged before being disbanded and ultimately destroyed. Unlike Poblet, Santes Creus is no longer fulfilling its original purpose but belongs to the Catalan government who have been responsible for all the restoration work. However, a number of the original buildings were converted into houses and now form a small village, with the abbot's palace occupied by the town hall. It overlooks a well proportioned square where there is a Baroque fountain dedicated to Sant Bernat Calbó. He was one of the more dedicated abbots and a counsellor to Jaume I who accompanied the king on his campaigns to recapture Valencia and Mallorca from the Moors.

The church overlooking the square has little in the way of decoration apart from an enormous Gothic window over the west door and a beautiful rose window, half hidden behind the high altar, still with some of its thirteenth-century glass. Two kings, Pedro II and his son Jaume II with his wife Blanche d'Anjou, are buried in moderate splendour, the former in a sarcophagus believed to have been carved by Master Bartomeu from a piece of prophyry inherited from the Romans. The chapter house is large and airy with the tombstones of various sixteenth-century abbots set into the floor and a stairway up to the dormitory which is now used as a concert hall.

The magnificent monastery of Santa Maria de Poblet

The cloister, with its beautifully manicured hedges, orange trees and roses, is surrounded by the tombs of members of the nobility and includes the lavabo in a Romanesque pavilion. Some of the intricate carving is the work of the English sculptor Reinald Fonoll who added what is thought to be a portrait of himself taking a rest against one of the columns in the company of a rather bemused cow. Parts of the royal palace have survived and so has the old chapel of the Trinity, turned into a parish church by an ex monk, Miguel Mestre, after the monastery was sacked; it is still used for daily services.

From the monastery, which overlooks the Río Gaià, framed by white poplars and hazel trees, a choice of minor roads explore the surrounding country with its woodlands, olive groves, vineyards and almond trees. There is nothing else of comparable historic interest in the immediate vicinity but plenty of opportunities to join the motorway south of Aiguamúrcia for a return visit to Barcelona or a trip to Lleida, 83km (51 miles) away in the opposite direction.

Additional Information

Places of Interest

Aiguamúrcia
Santes Creus Monastery
Open: 10am-12noon and 3.30-7pm April to September. 10am-12noon and 3.30-6pm October to March.
☎ Monastery 977 63 83 29. Parish 977 63 83 28.

L'Espluga de Francolí
Monastery of Santa Maria de Poblet
Open: 10am-12.30pm and 3-6pm March to August. 10am-12.30pm and 3-5.30pm September to February. Closed 25 December.
☎ Porter's Office 977 87 02 54.
Porter's Lodge 977 87 00 89.

Sitges
Casa Llopis Museum
Carrer Sant Josep
Open: 10am-1pm and 5-7pm April to September. 10am-1pm and 4-6pm October to March. Closed Sunday and some holidays.

Cau Ferrat Museum/Museu Maricel
Carrer Fonollar
Open: 10am-1.30pm and 4.30-6.30pm. Closed Monday and some holidays.

Tarragona
Museu Arqueològic
(Archaeological Museum)
Passeig de Sant Antoni
Open: 10am-2pm and 4-7pm.
10am-2pm Sunday. Closed Monday.

Museu Diocesano
(Cathedral Museum)
In the chapterhouse
Open: 10am-12noon and 4-7pm.
Closed Sunday mornings.

Museu d'Historia de Tarragona
Near the Archaeological Museum
Open: 10am-2pm and 4-7pm.
10am-2pm Sunday. Closed Monday.

Necropolis and Paleo-Christian Museum
Avinguda Ramón i Cajal
Open: 10am-1pm and 4.30-8pm.
10am-2pm Sunday.

Vilafranca del Penedés
Museu del Vi
Plaça Jaume I
Open: 10am-2pm and 4.30-7.30pm.
Closed Monday.

Vilanova i la Geltrú
Near Sitges
Balaguer Museum
Open: 11.30am-1.30pm and 3.30-8pm.

Casa Papiol
Open: 10am-1pm and 5-7pm June to mid-October. 10am-1pm and 4-6pm mid-October to May. 10am-2pm Sunday. Closed Sunday afternoon and Monday.

Castillo de la Geltrú
Open: 10am-1pm and 5-8pm April to September. 10am-1pm and 4-7pm October to March. Closed Monday except for holidays, 1 January, Good Friday, 1 May and Christmas.

Information Offices

Cambrils
Plaça Creu de Missió
Open: mid-June to mid-October.
☎ 977 36 11 59

Coma-ruga
Plaça Germans Trillas
☎ 977 68 00 10

L'Espluga de Francolí
Torres Jordi 16
☎ 977 74 04 56

Montblanc
Plaça de l'Ajuntament
☎ 977 86 00 09

Reus
Plaça Mercadal
☎ 977 30 57 40
or Sant Joan 36
☎ 977 31 00 61
or the Airport
(open: May to October).

Salou
Carrer Montblanc
☎ 977 38 01 36
or Espigó del Moll
☎ 977 38 00 33

Sitges
Passeig Vilafranca
☎ 93 894 12 30

Tarragona
Fortuny 4
☎ 977 23 34 15
or Major 39
☎ 977 23 89 22
or Plaça de la Font 1
☎ 977 23 48 12

Valls
Plaça del Blat 1
☎ 977 60 10 50

El Vendrell
Doctor Robert 33
☎ 977 66 02 92

4

THE DELTA DE L'EBRE

Strictly speaking, the Delta de l'Ebre is neither a costa nor a holiday playground. Nevertheless, it is an important and fascinating stretch of coast between the Golf de Sant Jordi and the Costa del Azahar which belongs to Castellón and Valencia. For the time being at least, the resorts of the Costa Daurada could be said to end at L'Hospitalet de l'Infant which is new, ambitious and probably destined for considerable highrise development in the near future. Beyond it is a low-lying area with pleasant sandy inlets surrounded by equally low-lying rocks and little human habitation before the fishing port of Ametlla de Mar. Here the fishing fleet has outgrown the harbour, leaving visiting yachtsmen to make for Ampolla which has already attracted a limited number of tourists but provides them with very little apart from two unremarkable campsites.

From Ampolla both the main road and the *autopista* take leave of the coast, the latter heading for Valencia while the former skirts round the delta to rejoin the sea at **Sant Carles de la Ràpita**. This small port was founded by Carlos III in 1780 and provided with a navigation canal in an unsuccessful attempt to open up the area. However, it is a pleasing little place with a fish market where the day's catch is auctioned off in the early evening and several small restaurants whose seafood dishes are highly recommended. Further inland, history begins to make itself felt in **Amposta**, the head-quarters of the Knights Hospitaller of Aragon in the twelfth century which boasts a ruined castle and a museum of natural history. Further south, Alcanar has a Moorish tower and some Iberian ruins while **Ulldecona**, on the far side of the motorway, delves even further back into the distant past with some modest rock paintings augmented by its own ancient church and fortress.

The Parc Natural del Delta de l'Ebre occupies most of the large, peninsula and is only second in size to the Doñana National Park at the mouth of the Guadalquivir south of Sevilla. In the days of the Moorish occupation it extended several miles out to sea but time and erosion have changed both its outline and several of its natural characteristics. The salty ground along the foreshore consists mainly of sand dunes and sparse vegetation edged with oleanders and tamarisk. The marshes are full of ponds bordered by reeds of various descriptions while the banks of the Ebre are lined with poplars and willows, backed up by species such as ash, elm, eucalyptus and even locust trees. Rice paddies give way to orchards and market gardens further inland but the park's main attraction is its enormous variety of wildlife including, unfortunately, the inevitable hordes of mosquitoes. Several of the larger animals like deer, wild boar and badgers have been leaving the area or simply dying out for some time but there are still a few otters and red foxes as well as weasels, wood mice and shrews. Fish are plentiful but they are outnumbered by the bird population, some of them only passing through while others are either permanent residents or visitors who, like their human counterparts, find it a good place to spend the winter. Apart from ducks, herons, egrets and gulls, the 300 or so different species include owls, avocets and flamingoes but few birds of prey.

Because of the threat from encroaching agricultural and tourist interest, the park was officially established in 1983 by the Generalitat de Catalunya which laid down a number of rules and regulations designed to protect the region without having to put it out of bounds to visitors. For example, camping is forbidden except on authorised sites or in special zones earmarked for the purpose. Sightseers are instructed to follow the marked paths, pay attention to 'No Entry' signs, keep dogs on their leads and not leave litter lying about. There are recommended points for photography and birdwatching as well as public ferries on the river and information centres that will provide everything from technical data or a visit to the Ecomuseum to specially conducted tours.

Tortosa, the principal town in the area, was originally a Roman settlement, captured by the Visigoths and later by the Moors but recovered in 1148 by Ramón Berenguer. It was strategically important because it guarded the only bridge over the Río Ebre but it managed to live a comparatively quiet life until 1938 when it got bogged down in the Civil War. The Republicans mounted a rear-guard attack on the Nationalist forces advancing on Valencia but were forced to dig themselves in, using trenches reminiscent of

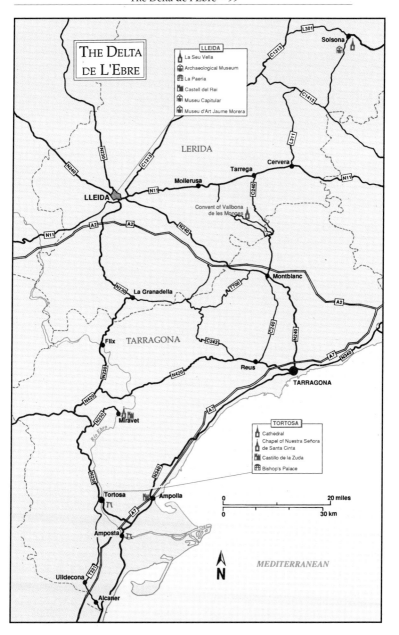

THE DELTA
DE L'EBRE

LLEIDA
La Seu Vella
Archaeological Museum
La Paeria
Castell del Rei
Museu Capitular
Museu d'Art Jaume Morera

LERIDA

Solsona

LLEIDA

Tarrega
Cervera
Mollerusa

Convent of Vallbona
de les Monges

TARRAGONA

La Granadella

Montblanc

Flix

Reus

TARRAGONA

Miravet

Río Ebro

TORTOSA
Cathedral
Chapel of Nuestra Señora
de Santa Cinta
Castillo de la Zuda
Bishop's Palace

Tortosa

Ampolla

0   20 miles
0   30 km

Amposta

Ulldecona

Alcaner

MEDITERRANEAN

N

World War I, and are reputed to have lost 150,000 men before being obliged to withdraw. A monument commemorating the battle was later built in the middle of the river, near the Plaça de Paiolet.

A short walk away is the all-but-completed cathedral, plain and a trifle severe but with some interesting touches inside. Foremost among them are a fourteenth-century carved wooden altarpiece depicting the Life of Christ and a font that apparently belonged to the medieval anti-pope Benedict XXIII. He ended his days somewhat ignominiously in the castle fortress at Peñiscola, across the border in Castellón. Meanwhile, the chapel of Nuestra Señora de Santa Cinta has its own special relic, a belt said to have belonged to the Virgin who is patron of the town. Just as viewable is the bishop's palace on the opposite side of the street. It has a fine Gothic chapel and spacious courtyard where a stairway taking up the whole of one wall leads in a straight line to the arcaded gallery above. The Castillo de la Zuda, which dominates both the town and the countryside bordering on the river, was built by the Moors to defend the delta region and converted into a Christian stronghold by the Templars during the twelfth century. Like so many of its kind, the castle was allowed to crumble but part of it has been restored and turned into an impressive *parador* with a memorable view. This extends right across to the rugged and seldom visited Ports de Beseit where the national hunting reserve is full of wild boar, mountain goats and ibex.

From Tortosa the N230 runs more or less beside the Ebre as far as El Pinell de Brai where it is demoted to a minor road for the last part of its journey to **Miravet**. This is a small hamlet overlooking the water with a disproportionately large castle perched on the top of a 300m (980ft) cliff. It is a strange, brooding medieval fortification given to the Knights Templar by Ramón Berenguer with instructions to guard the whole area. A narrow path leads up from the village to an ancient gateway in the massive walls. Beyond is the church of Sant Martí, built over a large vaulted space which may have been used as a storehouse or even as a stable. You can inspect the dormitory, the dining hall and the Patio de la Sang, so called because it was where the last of the Templars were beheaded in 1308. They had refused to obey the general instructions to disband their order, and were besieged and forced to surrender. Anyone with enough energy left can climb the spiral staircase in the tower to admire the view.

The N230 reappears on the far side of the N420, which links Reus with Alcañiz and Zaragoza, and makes its way to **Lleida**. This is the capital of Segrià, and is built on rising ground beside the Río Segre. It is another ancient city which, having been an Iberian capital, was promoted to a Roman municipality and subsequently became the centre of a small Moorish kingdom. After the Arabs were driven out in 1149, the Templars set about adapting it, 150 years later it was chosen as the site of the first Catalan university. Today it is an important agricultural town which still holds its traditional produce and livestock fair once a fortnight, as it has been doing for many hundreds of years.

The most outstanding thing about Lleida is La Suda with its enormous, partly Romanesque cathedral encased in Moorish walls, which is visible for miles around. Building started in 1203 and continued for nearly 200 years, during which it was given a lofty Gothic bell tower, a beautiful cloister and some most impressive stone carvings judging by the Porta dels Apòstols, the Porta des Fillols and sculptures of the Montcada family. Sadly, the cathedral was turned into a barracks during the Spanish War of Succession with dormitories constructed in the aisles, a kitchen in the cloister and target practice in the nave. Although it has been restored as far as possible, the Seu Vella, as it is known, has been replaced by a much less impressive cathedral not far from the river, complete with a small museum. It faces the former Hospital de Santa María, built in the fifteenth century, which is home to an archaeological museum with prehistoric finds.

Other places of interest in Lleida include the remains of the old Castell del Rei near the ancient cathedral and the thirteenth-century church of Sant Llorenç, and La Paeria, a solid, understated building with some lovely Romanesque windows. It has been home to the city's administrative departments since 1383 and now sets aside a few rooms for the Museu Arqueològic, a museum of history and archaeology. Additional attractions include medieval sculptures in the church of Sant Martí, Flemish tapestries in the Museu Capitular, weapons and coins in the Gabinet Numismatic i d'Armes and modern paintings by local artists gathered together in the Museu d'Art Jaume Morera. Most of them are hidden away in the tangle of little streets below the ancient walls between the Rambla d'Arago and the river but there is some archaeological digging in progress on the opposite side near the Portal de la Magdalena.

There are several attractive Modernist buildings, typified by the Casa Magi Llorenç, at the intersection of the Carrer Major and the Carrer de Cavallers, notable for its stone carving and quite elaborate wrought iron balconies. The Carrer Major and its extensions at either end have been turned into a pedestrian walkway, lined with a variety of little shops. However, there is no need to plod wearily up

A view over the rooftops of Tortosa

to the Seu Vella because a lift has been installed beside the Plaça de Sant Joan. It is also possible to drive up or hire a taxi in the town. Most of the local hotels are modest but reasonably well equipped, the largest and most comfortable of them being conveniently sited on the Carretera de Barcelona which is another name for the N11, on the opposite side of the river. There are also two campsites in the vicinity, both seasonal and neither with bungalows to rent.

Motorists in a hurry can head due south from Lleida to join the Barcelona motorway but there is also a good, if slightly longer route through Mollerusa to **Cervera** where a tunnel enables most of the traffic to bypass the town. However, it is worth spending a little time inspecting the church of Sant Pere le Gros, an unusual circular

The Castillo de la Zuda dominates Tortosa's skyline

building that was once part of a Benedictine monastery, and the church of Santa María whose south door belonged to its predecessor and shows St Martin giving part of his cloak to a beggar. Sections of the old walls built at the time of Pedro III are still standing but most visitors make straight for the old university. It was founded in 1718 by Philip V in a futile attempt to combine all the Catalan universities under one roof, half way between those of Barcelona and Lleida. In 1841 all the students were moved out again, leaving the deserted building to fill its empty halls with archives belonging to the regional press of Catalunya. Outwardly it has not changed at all and still wears a massive crown over the entrance. This was a silent protest, designed to show that the whole unfortunate episode was not a local blunder but the result of a royal decree.

Solsona, tucked away in the mountains to the north, is also worthy of attention. It is a typical walled survivor from the Middle Ages that has retained its ruined castle and the cathedral of Santa María. This achieved its present status in 1593 when the former monastery church became the seat of a bishopric. Restored and updated several times since then, it is rather dark and subdued with little to hold your attention apart from the famous black stone Virgin of the cloister. However, the bishop's palace next door is another matter altogether. It is filled to capacity with all manner of exhibits, some of them marginally out of place in a Diocesan Museum. The displays of sacred art include a splendid collection of altarfronts, paintings from Sant Pere de Casserres, near Vic, several frescoes and a twelfth-century version of the Apocalypse. In a slightly different vein, the prehistoric gallery has an attractive range of pottery while the Salt Museum consists entirely of articles carved out of salt from nearby Cardona, where it has been mined since Roman times. The old quarter of the town is extremely picturesque; full of narrow streets, old mansions and fifteenth-century fountains. The Ethnographical Museum has collected a host of everyday items and has given them an appropriate setting in one of the old houses.

The vast plain surrounding Lleida is exceptionally fertile, speckled with agricultural hamlets producing cereals, olives, almonds, vegetables and large quantities of fruit. The Romans constructed irrigation canals which the Moors perfected during their 400 year term of office. The Arabs' highly efficient system of interlocking furrows resulted in ideal farming conditions which made it relatively simple for the large Cistercian monasteries like Poblet to create their own thriving rural communities. The Cistercian nuns were often as deeply involved in this type of project as the monks.

The most important convent in the region was, and still is, Santa María de Vallbona de les Monges, south of Tarrega. It was established in the twelfth century when both Alfonso I and Jaume I took it under their royal wings and kept a well informed eye on the building work. The abbey church runs true to form with an elegant octagonal lantern and the tombstones of various abbesses, but these are somewhat overshadowed by the tombs of Queen Violant of Hungary, who married Jaume I, and her daughter Sancha of Aragon; both buried in the sanctuary. The cloister is an oddly attractive mixture of styles, ranging from aggressively plain and Romanesque to lavishly decorated Gothic with star-shaped rose windows, no doubt inspired by the Arabs. It contrasts sharply with the chapter house which is extremely dark and almost painfully austere. The convent lost its outer precincts at the time when nuns were forbidden to hide themselves away in isolated spots so a small lay community moved in to keep them company. This is why there are two arches standing forlornly in one of the village streets when, in fact, they should be holding up the roof of a cellar. The former burial ground is now a square with a monumental fountain, a number of tombs and sarcophagi and an arresting Door of the Dead which once led into the choir.

Apart from establishing farms that gradually grew into villages, Vallbona ran an exclusive school for the daughters of the nobility, a hospital for the poor and a large hostelry where travellers and pilgrims were always welcome. It managed to survive the upheavals of the early nineteenth century, but its occupants were reduced from about 150 nuns, with all their lay sisters and servants, to a compliment of little more than thirty. Nevertheless, it still runs a guest house, and maintains both a library and a small museum full of gold and silverware, statues, embroidery and a most unusual collection of ancient pills and potions. It also holds summer concerts in the church. Although Vallbona de les Monges is a little out on a limb, situated in a valley surrounded by farms and woodland, it is only a short distance from the motorway and the main road to Tarragona. As a result, it makes an interesting and enjoyable day's outing for holidaymakers in search of a change from the sun, sea and sand of the Costa Daurada.

Additional Information

Places of Interest

Cervera
Old University
Enquire at the entrance or from the Mairie.

Lleida
Gabinet Numismatic i d'Armes
Carrer del Carme 26
☎ 973 23 57 45

Museu Arqueològic
(Archaeological Museum)
Plaça de la Catedral
☎ 973 27 15 00

Museu Capitular
Plaça de la Catedral
☎ 973 22 15 20

Museu de la Paeria
Plaça de la Paeria
Enquire for all opening times at the Tourist Office (see below).

Museu Diocesà d'Escultura Medieval
Carrer Jaume el Conqueridor 67
☎ 973 22 15 20

Seu Vella
On the hilltop
Open: 10am-2pm and 3.30-6pm
Tuesday to Saturday. 9am-2pm
and 4-8pm Sunday. Closed
Monday.

Miravet
Templar Castle
Enquire at the Mairie, or the
Tourist Office (see below for
telephone number).

Parc Natural del Delta de l'Ebre
Information Office
Plaça del 20 de maig, Deltebre. In
the centre of the park.
Open: during office hours.
☎ 977 48 95 11

Ornithological Centre
Open: 10am-1pm Friday and
Saturday.

Solsona
Diocesan Museum
In the bishop's palace
Open: 10am-1pm and 4.30-7pm
May to September. 10am-1pm and
4-6pm October to April. Closed
Monday, 1 January and 25
December.

Ethnographical Museum
Enquire at the Tourist Office (see
below) but normally open 10am-
1pm and 4-7pm.

Vallbona de les Monges Convent
South of Tarrega
Open: 10am-2pm and 4.30-7.30pm
weekdays. 12noon to 2pm and
4.30-7.30pm Sunday and public
holidays. Times of masses: 8.30am
weekdays and 11am Sundays and
public holidays.
☎ 973 33 02 66

Tourist Offices

Lleida
Arc del Pont
☎ 973 24 81 20
or 973 24 02 00

Miravet
Casnal
☎ 977 40 72 39

Solsona
Castell 20
☎ 973 48 00 50 or 973 48 23 61

Tortosa
Plaça d'Espanya
☎ 977 44 00 00

5

COSTA DEL AZAHAR

There is no better description of this long, shallow, gently curving bay than the 'Orange Blossom Coast'. The Costa del Azahar stretches from the Catalan border down the shoreline of Castellón to the city of Valencia and then sweeps out into the Mediterranean to meet the Costa Blanca just short of Denia. It is a low-lying area whose sandy beaches are interspersed with pebbles and an occasional rocky outcrop, backed by one of the most fertile regions in the country. The rugged terrain in the north-western corner, which spills over into Aragon, contrasts sharply with the extensive rice fields round Valencia and La Albufera, the largest freshwater lagoon in Spain. However, the vast citrus orchards create the most lasting impression, spreading out on either side of the main road and the motorway in a sea of dark green leaves, gold and yellow fruit and delicate white blossom that scents the air for many miles.

The Costa del Azahar changed hands at frequent intervals, playing host to the Phoenicians, the Greeks, the Romans and the Moors, among other invaders. It was recaptured by the Christians in the thirteenth century, took up arms against the Bourbons during the War of Succession and sided with the government against Franco at the outbreak of the Civil War. Today it is an autonomous region, similar to Catalunya, with a large population, a thriving economy, its own local language and innumerable tourist attractions.

Driving down from Sant Carlos de la Ràpita on the Delta de l'Ebre, the first place of any size is **Vinaròs**. It is an important fishing port with a sprinkling of unremarkable hotels and restaurants and three local campsites. There is a pleasant beach offering a variety of water sports, an eighteenth-century church and a direct link with Morella in the mountainous region known as El Maestrazgo.

Like many of the surrounding hamlets, **Morella** was fortified by the Knights of Montesa during their battles with the Moors and is certainly one of the most spectacular of all these ancient strongholds. The typical village with its narrow streets and whitewashed houses clambers laboriously up the hillside to the ruins of a medieval castle whose nearest neighbour is an old Franciscan monastery with a beautiful thirteenth-century cloister. The Basilica de Santa María la Mayor is an outstanding example of Gothic architecture, memorable chiefly for its spiral staircase, stained-glass windows, carved door-ways and ornate sanctuary. The whole village is enclosed in massive walls pierced by fortified gateways, the most imposing of which is the Puerta de San Miguel. Accommodation in the village is some-what limited, especially during the feast of Corpus Christi when crowds watch the processions which are basically religious in character but have various traditional hangers-on in the form of giants, dwarfs, devils and dancers.

There is really no alternative route leading directly back to the coast although a minor road branches off to **Benicarló**, a neat and understated little resort with a modern *parador*, comfortable apart-ments attached to one of the other hotels, two pleasing beaches and a fairly viewable church. From here a fairly scenic road follows the shoreline down to **Peñiscola** which is sometimes described as the pearl of the Costa del Azahar. It is a well fortified medieval town, built on a small peninsula, with the nucleus of a large holiday playground. The Phoenicians are said to have been the first people to have occupied the site, followed by the Romans, the Carthaginians and the Moors, but it was the Templars who built Macho Castle, a formidable fortress stretched out along the top of the promontory. Its most colourful resident was Benedict XIII, the last anti-pope, who was born Pedro de Luna in Aragon in 1338. Slightly more than half a century later he was elected by his fellow cardinals in Avignon to succeed Clement VII but when he lost the support of the French king and was accused of heresy, Papa Luna chose to cut and run rather than abdicate. He took refuge in the castle, had his coat-of-arms emblazoned on one of the gates and remained here until his death in 1423. The fortress has been much restored since the days of Papa Luna. However, his memory lingers on in the church, the enormous hall and his private study in the tower where, among other things, he confirmed the foundation of St Andrew's University in Scotland.

Peñiscola is well supplied with hotels and campsites, and has its full quota of atmospheric little streets. There are also two extensive beaches, and the town is flooded with souvenirs during the summer.

So far it is possible to walk but not drive along the foreshore to **Alcoceber** which has nothing of historic interest to offer but makes up for this omission with no fewer than three different beaches, freshwater springs and opportunities for sailing and windsurfing. A short byway connects it to the main road near Torreblanca which has its own beach some 3km (2 miles) away, attached to a small fishing harbour.

Another minor road, slightly to the north, circles round the ruined fortress at Alcalá de Chivert and then heads off through orchards and olive groves to join the C238 on the outskirts of **Cuevas de Vinroma**. In common with several other places in the area, this village has a residue of prehistoric rock paintings and its own version of the Stations of the Cross. For a brief moment during World War II it attracted publicity when it was claimed that the Virgin had appeared to certain pilgrims on more than one occasion, assuring them of a German victory over both the Russians and the Jews. When this turned out to be nothing more than wishful thinking the whole fabrication died a sudden death, and the hamlet retreated into its habitual obscurity.

The main coastal highway has very little contact with the sea between Benicarló and Oropesa, with its ruins, before heading down through Benicasim to **Castellón de la Plana**, the fairly industrial capital of the northern region. It is a pleasant, friendly centre which was moved down to its present position on the plain from a nearby cliff in the thirteenth century. Castellón suffered badly during the Civil War, after which the cathedral had to be rebuilt. However, the city has gathered together some paintings and local arts and crafts which are displayed in the Art Museum on the Calle Caballeros. Regardless of the fact that it is short of historic buildings and atmospheric little alleys, Castellón is popular with tourists and visitors alike and celebrates with infectious gaiety on every suitable occasion. Its holiday accommodation includes two comfortable hotels, one near the Plaza de la Paz and the other at El Grao, the port area 5km (3 miles) away where there is a sailing club, the nine hole Costa de Azahar golf course and a fine, long, sandy beach. Some 43km (27 miles) out to sea the Islas Columbretes, a collection of minute volcanic islands, attract underwater fishermen and divers from resorts all along the coast. Special excursions are laid on from Oropresa during the holiday season.

Inland from the capital there is the eighteen hole Club de Golf Campo del Mediterraneo at La Coma but nothing else of interest apart from **Villafamés**, a small but delightful hill village full of

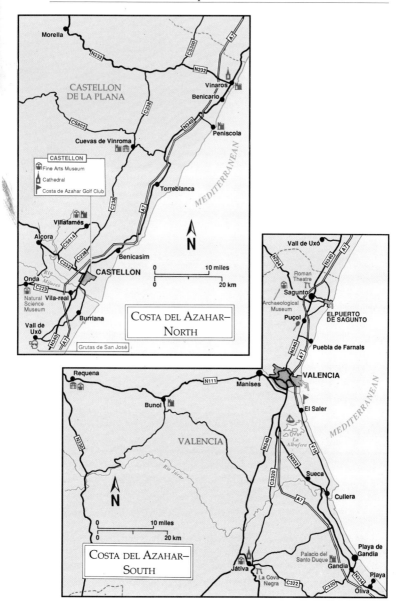

Morella
N232
CS300
A7
CASTELLON
DE LA PLANA
N232
Vinaros
Benicarlo
C238
CS802
N340
Peniscola
Cuevas de Vinroma
CASTELLON
Fine Arts Museum
Cathedral
Costa de Azahar Golf Club
Torreblanca
MEDITERRANEAN
C238
A7
Villafamés
N
Alcora
CS814
C232
C229
Benicasim
Río Mijares
CASTELLON
10 miles
0
Onda
C223
0
20 km
Natural
Science
Museum
Vila-real
Burriana
COSTA DEL AZAHAR–
Vall de
Uxó
N340
A7
NORTH
Grutas de San José

Vall de Uxó
N234
A7
Roman
Theatre
Sagunto
Archaeological
Museum
N340
EL PUERTO
DE SAGUNTO
Puçol
N340
A7
Puebla de Farnals

Requena
N111
Manises
VALENCIA
MEDITERRANEAN
Bunol
El Saler
N330
VALENCIA
La
Albufera
N
V15
Río Júcar
N340
N332
C3320
Sueca
10 miles
0
A7
Cullera
0
20 km
COSTA DEL AZAHAR–
SOUTH
Playa de
Gandia
Palacio del
Santo Duque
Játiva
Gandia
N332
Playa
La Cova
Negra
C322
C320
Oliva

The Basilica de Santa María in Morella is well worth a visit

The exterior of Benicarló's Iglesia de San Bartolome

cobbled streets lined with old houses. It is extremely proud of both the ruins of its ancient castle and a fifteenth-century mansion which is used for a Museum of Contemporary Art. Still to the north of the Río Mijares, with its scattered collection of man-made lakes, the slightly larger town of Alcora is the place to go in search of souvenirs. It has been perfecting its ceramic art work for well over 200 years, unlike **Onda**, on the opposite side of the river, which does not bother much with decorative designs, preferring to point visitors in the direction of its enterprising El Carmen Natural Science Museum. A straight road leads out past the ruined Castle of Three Hundred Towers, whose name must have been a bit of an overstatement even when it was intact, and carries on straight through the expanse of orange trees to **Vila-real**. Here the main reason for stopping is to inspect the enormous parish church which has series of paintings tracing the life and work of St James, the Apostle.

From here onwards the main route continues its journey south with hardly a glance to left or right, although it does send out tentative feeler roads to various little seaside resorts where they end abruptly at the water's edge. Most of these miniscule *playas* are attached to their own parent villages a few kilometres inland which, in turn, are mostly surrounded by orange groves, pine woods and rice paddies. **Burriana** is rather bigger than most because it is a commercial centre with a busy port whereas Nules, Moncofar and Chilches have difficulty in providing one campsite apiece. However, they all have an ever-growing number of holiday villas and appropriately ambitious plans for the near future. The only diversion in this area is a collection of caves known as the Grutas de San José near Vall de Uxó, hollowed out by an underground river, where a short boat trip enables visitors to examine the illuminated rock formations.

Sagunto, just across the border in the province of Valencia, was the scene of an epic struggle in 219BC. The Carthaginians, led by Hannibal, laid siege to what was then a small seaport with Roman affiliations. The defenders held out for several months but when it became obvious that Rome had abandoned them, they built an enormous fire inside the walls. The women and children and anyone else who was unable to fight threw themselves onto it while the rest of the citizens broke out for one last battle against the enemy. Five years later the Romans recaptured the town but eventually lost it to the Visigoths who were succeeded in due course by the Moors and then by the Christians. All these invaders left traces of their occupation, especially in the acropolis with its massive walls and miscellaneous collection of ruins covering several centuries.

The Romans' most lasting contribution is the theatre, also on the hillside above the town. It has been extremely well restored, has a modern lighting system, and provides enough space for an audience of 8,000 on the semi-circle of stone tiers. These are cold and uncomfortable without a cushion but have an uninterrupted view of both the stage and the sea. Next door is the Archaeological Museum, housing a variety of discoveries made in the vicinity, none of them very noteworthy except for the Iberian bull. Among the other attractions are two elderly churches, some ancient houses and the old Jewish quarter with its steep and narrow streets.

Sagunto has its own beaches 5km (3 miles) away, beyond which are one or two isolated little seaside developments in addition to **Puçol**, just a fraction inland and easily accessible from the motorway. It has an upmarket hotel, a casino and sports facilities ranging from riding stables, tennis courts and swimming pools to a bullring where amateur matadores are given a chance to prove themselves. El Puig, quite close by, has a seventh-century monastery whereas Puebla de Farnals is a largely modern development. It has apartment blocks, a yacht club and moorings for pleasure craft but little accommodation for tourists who are simply passing through.

Valencia itself is a busy, extrovert city with plenty to offer its visitors. It has a lengthy history but is not as old as Sagunto, having been founded in 138BC by the Romans for some disgruntled legionaries. Their descendants took up arms against Pompey who taught them a severe lesson in 75BC. The Visigoths who came afterwards were not much help either so it was left to the Moors to usher in an age of peace and plenty. They irrigated the surrounding countryside and started up a number of profitable industries including papermaking, the manufacture of silk after their mulberry trees began to flourish, glass and leather crafts, pottery and metalwork. However, this prosperity did not last.

In 1094, after a long siege, Valencia surrendered to Rodrigo Días de Vivar, better known as El Cid, who signed a capitulation agreement with ibn Yehhaf and then characteristically went back on his word and murdered him. The Arabs made two unsuccessful attempts to redress the balance but it was not until 3 years after the death of El Cid in 1099 that his widow Jimena was forced to capitulate. The city was recaptured by Jaume I in 1238 and some 250 years later passed into the hands of Ferdinand II along with Catalunya, Aragon and Mallorca. Things were going quite well until the early seventeenth century when a decision was taken to expel all the remaining Moors and Jews. This had disastrous consequences, including almost total

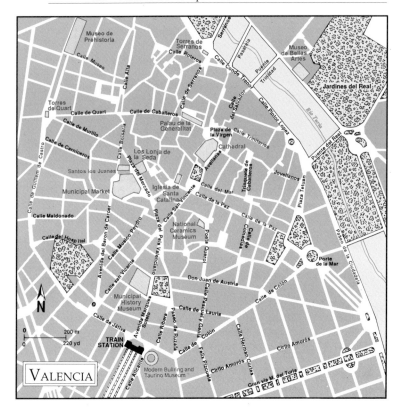

VALENCIA

economic collapse, epitomising Valencia's turbulent past and regular involvement in conflict, almost invariably on the losing side. The last occasion was during the Civil War when it became the seat of the Republican Government for a short period after the fall of Madrid and therefore a prime target for the Nationalist bombers who badly damaged the old town.

Ideally, a sightseeing tour of Valencia starts at the cathedral, built on the site of a former mosque between the thirteenth and fifteenth centuries and backing onto the lovely Plaza de la Virgen which may well have been the old Roman forum. It is a predictable mixture of styles but, despite this, it can spring an odd surprise or two, such as the Star of David which fills the large rose window above the decorative Puerta de los Apóstoles. It is here, out in the open air, that the famous Tribunal de las Aguas, or Water Court, meets every

Locals in Castellón de la Plana preparing a traditional dish

The House of Shells, Peñiscola

Thursday to sit in judgment on any disputes to do with matters of irrigation in the province. The eight members, representing the areas supplied by the various independent canals, weigh up all the evidence, pass sentence on the guilty and impose an appropriate fine. Nothing is written down and there is no appeal, which may sound a bit arbitrary in this day and age but the system has been working perfectly for more than 1,000 years and nobody has come up with a better or fairer alternative.

The interior of the cathedral has been considerably restored since 1939 and is suitably decorative although most of the treasures, apart from one or two items, are kept in the museum. A special chapel has been set aside for the Saint Chalice, or Holy Grail, which the Knights of the Round Table searched for long and diligently, without success. According to the legend, the cup used at the Last Supper was taken to Rome, probably by St Peter, but some 300 years later was sent to the monastery of San Juan de la Peña, in Huesca, to keep it safe from Valerian. From there it passed into the kings of Aragon's hands; one of whom gave it to Valencia cathedral in 1473. During the nineteenth century the holy relic went missing again and was only returned to the cathedral in 1939. The chalice consists of a small, dark, purplish-red agate bowl standing on a gold and jewel-encrusted base dating from the fourteenth century. Apparently, the relic was examined minutely by Antonio Beltran, the professor of archaeology at Zaragoza University, in about 1960. He obviously could not confirm the truth of the legend but said that, in his opinion, the bowl had been made in the Middle East and was certainly old enough to have been used at the Last Supper.

At one end of the cathedral is a tall, octagonal tower, known affectionately as El Micalet, which has a formidable array of bells and a splendid view. At the other end is the Basilica de Nuestra Señora de los Desamparados. It is widely believed that the statue of Our Lady of the Deserted was made by angels disguised as pilgrims and left as a present for the city which immediately adopted her as its patron. Every spring she is carried in procession through the streets while crowds lining the route cover her path with flowers. Other churches of note in the vicinity include the Iglesia de Santa Catalina with a tower that is claimed to be the most beautiful of its kind in Spain, and beyond it, just off the Calle de la Paz, the collegiate church founded by Bishop Juan Ribera. Apart from a modern statue of Ribera in the patio, there are some interesting fifteenth-century Flemish tapestries, a sizeable range of frescoes and glazed tiles and a small museum. It contains some quite noteworthy paintings as well as a Book of Miniatures which show that golf was a popular sport in royal circles during the Middle Ages.

The old Palau de la Generalitat of the Kingdom of Valencia is now occupied by the provincial council. It faces the Plaza de la Virgen and contains the Salón Dorado and Salón de Cortes. The latter is decorated with sixteenth-century murals. The National Ceramics Museum is conveniently situated in the somewhat over-decorated Dos Aguas Palace two or three blocks away. Among the several thousand exhibits, going back to Iberian times, are thirteenth-century examples from Paterna, which produced green and white ware with brown manganese streaks that was all the rage in its day. It vies for attention with lustred pottery from Manises that was exported to places as far apart as London, Cairo and the Crimea 500 and more years ago. Other sections are devoted to Oriental porcelain, Picasso creations and an extremely colourful Valencian kitchen, not to mention the Marqués de Dos Aguas' eighteenth-century carriage, parked firmly on the ground floor.

The Plaza del Ayuntamiento, a favourite haunt of flower-sellers and souvenir stallkeepers, is overlooked by the post office and the modern city hall, built in traditional style with a clock tower, domes and sculptures, providing both administrative offices and a home for the Municipal History Museum. The exhibits range from a sword that Jaume I took into battle and the banner which inspired his troops during the reconquest, to a map of Valencia as it was at the end of the seventeenth century. Also on display are ancient books and documents and a collection of pictures. Meanwhile the Taurino Museum, part of the modern bullring down the road next to the station, insists that it is one of the oldest, most valuable and most comprehensive of its kind in the country. It is full of bullfighting memorabilia and has some interesting and eye-catching exhibits.

In the past bullfights were staged in the Plaza del Mercado, within a few blocks of the cathedral. Here the two most elderly attractions are the large medieval church of Los Santos Juanes, considerably updated some 200 years ago and badly damaged by fire in the Civil War, and the Lonja de la Seda, or Silk Exchange. It was specially built for the purpose towards the end of the fifteenth century and is worth seeing for the main hall with its twisted pillars and stone tracery in the bays, as well as the ceiling in the Salon del Consulado del Mar, approached up a stairway from the Orange Tree Court. The third occupant of the square, and no less striking in its own way, is the municipal market. This is an enormous modern construction with room for more than a thousand stalls, and is filled with local produce.

A bridge spans the old course of the Turia river in Valencia

Flowersellers in the Plaza del Ayuntamiento, Valencia

In its earlier days Valencia was a fortified city surrounded by Roman walls rebuilt by Pedro IV in 1356. Unfortunately these were pulled down just over 100 years ago. However, two of the gates were left standing — the Torres de Quart used by travellers from Castile and the Torres de Serranos; somewhat larger, slightly older and a fine example of proven military architecture in the Middle Ages. Beyond the area where the walls stood, a series of bridges span what was once the Río Turia whose main stream was diverted in 1957 and replaced with an elongated park. On the far side is the Museo de Bellas Artes (Fine Arts Museum) which has some very viewable exhibits such as a self-portrait by Velázquez, El Greco's *St John the Baptist* and many examples of contemporary art. It stands on one corner of the Jardines del Real (former Royal Gardens), a delightfully shaded area full of sculptures and roses that once surrounded the kings' palace but now provides the setting for a small zoo.

There are many other churches and museums dotted about the old city but by far the most original is the Fallas Museum on the Plaza Monteolivete. In the Middle Ages the carpenters of Valencia used to celebrate the feast of their patron saint, St Joseph, on 19 March, by making bonfires with all their sawdust and unwanted bits of wood. This coincided with the advent of spring and before long the habit developed into a ritual and a fairly safe opportunity for criticism and ridicule. Artists started making effigies which gradually developed into set pieces and set them up at street intersections and in the most important squares, ready for the Night of Fire. Today the fallas are big business. Hollow wooden frames are covered with modelling clay and moulded into the desired shapes, which can be anything from a pompous official to an historic scene, a famous picture, a cartoon or a mythical animal. These are filled with wet pasteboard that is left to dry out before being removed and painted. Some of the fallas are valued at several million pesetas and can be up to three or four storeys high, made in sections and assembled for the festivities that begin at dawn on 15 March. Each creation has its own group of attendants and sometimes a band. The climax comes after dark on St Joseph's Day when all the fallas go up in smoke, accompanied by fire crackers and a massive fireworks display. Only one, judged to be the best or the most amusing, is spared and this lone survivor is trans-ferred to the Fallas Museum to act as an inspiration for the following year. The collection covers more than 50 years.

Valencia has many other interests, many of which are commercial such as heavy industry, petrochemicals and printing, a profession that goes back to 1474 when the first printing press was set up in the city. It is also an important agricultural centre, has a busy port and souvenir shops which are filled with ceramics, lace and attractive fans. The botanical gardens on the Calle Beato Gaspar Bono, near the river, are said to be among the first of their type in Spain and are home to thousands of different kinds of plants as well as very viewable collections of molluscs and butterflies. Meanwhile, the Ethnological Museum, a few blocks away, concentrates on clothes and furniture, kitchen utensils, agricultural equipment and traditional arts and crafts, leaving the prehistoric section to deal with archaeology.

Valencia goes to considerable trouble to keep its guests entertained. It has an aeroclub, a yacht club with berths for visitors, golf courses, tennis courts, riding stables and official centres where information can be obtained about hunting, fishing or mountaineering. Popular spectator sports include the Carreras de Joies, (horse racing) and three different variations of pelota. In the evening there are night clubs and discos, flamenco shows, cabarets and a music hall as well as gambling in the casino at Puçol which stays open until 5am on Fridays, Saturdays and on the evening before a public holiday.

The city is justifiably proud of its traditional recipes, especially paella which was invented here in the middle of the nineteenth century. Among a host of other special rice dishes are some calling for snails and spinach or squid and cauliflower. Eels are grilled or roasted and served with a sauce made from garlic, olive oil and paprika, followed by a choice of sweets like roasted almonds or chestnuts with a sugar coating. Drinks range from local wines to *horchata*, a concoction made from *chufas*, or earth almonds, that is particularly refreshing in hot weather.

Gunpowder, fire and music are among the main ingredients for many traditional festivals as well as the fallas, some harking back to pagan times while others are more recent innovations like the feast of San Dionís, commemorating the reconquest of the city by Jaume I. At times like this it is essential to book accommodation well in advance — although Valencia has plenty of hotels in every category, it is almost impossible to find a room of any description at the last moment.

Travelling to, from and around Valencia is very simple. The international airport is less than 10km (6 miles) from the city and there are frequent trains to Madrid and other places as far afield as Bilbao and Sevilla. Scheduled coach services keep in constant touch with several European countries, augmented by buses to other provincial capitals and leading holiday resorts. The city buses run from 5.30am until 11pm, with what is called a 'night owl' service on specially selected routes, in addition to which there are plenty of taxis and cars for hire. There are ferries operating to Mallorca and Ibiza with longer voyages to the Canary Islands.

Despite the two local beaches just north of the harbour, with the usual selection of cafés and restaurants, most visitors prefer one of the nearby resorts like **El Saler** where there is a modern *parador*, a long sandy beach and a beautiful eighteen hole golf course. It backs on to **La Albufera**, a vast expanse of freshwater cut off from the sea by a narrow strip of sand covered with pine trees. Surrounded by orchards and rice paddies, it is a favourite spot with hunters after wildfowl in the autumn and fishermen in their traditional sailing boats looking for eels. Boats can be hired in one of the adjoining villages like Silla but there are no set tariffs at the moment so it may be necessary to haggle or even try elsewhere if the initial asking price seems too high. The late afternoon is the best time to venture out when the atmosphere and the constantly changing colours are a sheer delight.

There are not many places to visit on the plain that extends inland from La Albufera to the foothills of the Corbera Sierra but the drive through farmlands, vineyards and woods to the plateau round **Requena** makes a very pleasant outing. The town, surrounded by vineyards and pine forests, has preserved a small palace that once belonged to El Cid, another associated with the Inquisition, and two medieval churches. Remnants of the original walls are still standing and the keep has been restored and refurbished to make space for the Wine and Archaeological Museums. It is very easy to drive from Valencia to Requena along the main N111 road to Madrid with the option of turning off to **Manises**, the ancient pottery town where some of the workshops are open to visitors. The main road carries on to Chiva and then Buñol, dominated by its ancient Moorish castle, with an alternative route back through Dos Aguas where there are two prehistoric shelters with a few modest cave paintings.

Most of the small seaside resorts strung out along the coast below La Albufera can provide somewhere to pitch a tent or park a caravan, with a first class site at Sueca, open throughout the year, and another at **Cullera** which has bungalows to rent. The latter is a smallish port on the mouth of the Río Júcar; it has a series of highrise blocks along the edge of an open bay with a lighthouse at the northern end. Apart from all the usual sports facilities, there is a comfortable hotel on the road to the lighthouse with what amounts to its own stretch of beach, a number of smaller but reasonably well equipped establishments and a particularly good restaurant not far from the ruined castle. The hermitage of Nuestra Señora del Castillo stands a little aloof from the resort itself, perched on the hillside with two old churches for company and a very worthwhile view.

From Cullera a secondary road joins the main route to the south with a turning off shortly afterwards to **Játiva** which has much of interest in terms of both history and architecture. It was the birthplace of two Borgia popes, Calixtus III who was Bishop of Valencia, and his nephew Rodrigo who made his mark as the infamous Alexander VI. Ever since Játiva was founded by the Moors on Mount Vernisa, the highest point of the area, the townspeople have proved extremely hostile. Things came to a head in 1707 when Philip V lost patience with them, captured the town, partly demolished the fortress, set fire to several of the buildings and rechristened the remainder San Felipe in the hope of bringing the citizens to heel. However, this so-called 'town of a thousand fountains' soon reverted to its Arab name, set about restoring the damage and refused to change its general attitude, thereby creating fresh problems during the Civil War.

Today Játiva is highly respectable, the capital of the region and one of the most picturesque hill towns in the province of Valencia. The remaining ramparts, which so offended Philip V, still keep watch over the surrounding countryside while the old and the new quarters face each other across a modern avenue. The hermitage of Sant Feliú, once a Visigoth cathedral but updated in the thirteenth century, stands just outside the walls on the road up to the castle. It is older though not as imposing as the enormous collegiate church on the Plaza del Seo which was damaged by fire in the 1930s but managed to save a fair number of its prize possessions, some of which were gifts from the Borgias.

An old granary on the Carrer de la Corretgera has been converted into the Municipal Museum and divides its attention between archaeological discoveries and paintings by José Ribera. He was born in Játiva at the end of the sixteenth century but settled in Naples where he became known as Lo Spagnoletto, or 'The Little Spaniard'. He produced some of his most startling work under the patronage of the Duke of Osuna, who was the Spanish viceroy in Naples for several years, but mellowed considerably towards the end of his life. Other attractions on offer include the hospital with its attractive façade, a Gothic aqueduct, the prehistoric excavation site of La Cova Negra and the observation platform of El Bellveret. The local hotels are disappointing so the best plan for anyone looking for somewhere

Cullera's bay is surrounded by high-rise hotels

The courtyard of Gandia's Palacio del Santo Duque

to spend the night would probably be to head for Gandia, a developing seaside resort nearby.

Gandia is also closely associated with the Borgias, having been given to the family by King Ferdinand in 1485. However, the town prefers to overlook the misdemeanours of Pope Alexander, ignores both his offspring, Lucretia and Caesar, and skips the next generation to focus its attention on the fourth duke, Francis Borgia, who was born in the castle in 1510. For many years he was an equerry at the court of the Emperor Charles V but after the death of his wife he joined the Society of Jesus and was ordained 5 years later. Leaving all his estates to be handled by his son, Francis set about establishing the Jesuit Order throughout western Europe and across the Atlantic in the Americas. The missionaries worked tirelessly among the Indians and even gained a measure of control in Paraguay. As the vicar general he made his headquarters in Rome where he died at the age of 62 and was canonised in 1671. The Palacio del Santo Duque, where St Francis was born, is now a Jesuit college, extensively modernised at quite frequent intervals but still retaining a number of ornate apartments and some sixteenth-century frescoes. There are several relics of this member of the Borgias, including his personal crucifix which is kept in one of the chapels.

The collegiate church was raised to its present status by Alexander Borgia from more modest beginnings in the fourteenth century, when it grew up alongside the monastery of Santa Clara and San Marcos Hospital, to be followed about 200 years later by the university. While making the most of all its historic associations, Gandia pays just as much attention to its current role as a popular holiday playground. There are several hotels, including a first class one near the seafront, a number of restaurants, three good campsites and a marina attached to the Club Nautico. The beaches are wide, sandy and usually overcrowded at the height of the season when people in search of a little more room to move about have started creating similar conditions at **Oliva**, about 8km (5 miles) down the coast. The town stands back some 3km (2 miles) from the foreshore and is a pleasant, unprepossessing little place which shares Gandia's interest in oranges but has not yet developed any industrial tendencies. About ten different campsites compensate for the lack of hotels, especially as half of them have bungalows as well. Oliva's generally calm, clear stretch of the Mediterranean continues down as far as the Río Molinell which separates the Costa del Azahar from the Costa Blanca on the opposite bank.

Additional Information

Places of Interest

Castellón de la Plana
Art Museum
Calle Caballeros
Open: 3-8pm on weekdays. 10am-1pm Saturday.

Gandia
Palacio del Santo Duque
Open: 10am-12noon and 5-7pm May to September. 11am-12noon and 4.30-5.30pm October to April.

Grutas de San José
Near Vall de Uxó
Open: 10am-1pm and 3-5pm. May stay open later during the summer.

Játiva
Castle remains
Open: 10am-2pm and 4.30-8pm. Closed Monday.

Collegiate Church
Open: 9-10am and 6.30-8pm.

Municipal Museum
Carrer de la Corretgeria
Open: 10am-2pm. Tuesday to Saturday.

Morella
Basilica de Santa María la Mayor
Open: 11am-2pm and 3.30-6pm.

Onda
El Carmen Natural Science Museum
In the south-west of the town.
Open: 9.30am-2pm and 3.30-8pm June to September. Closes earlier out of season, also Monday and 20 December until 6 January.

Peñiscola
Fortress
Open: 10am-8pm in summer. Otherwise 10am-1pm and 4.15-6.30pm.

Requena
Wine and Archaeological Museums
In the castle keep.
Enquire at the municipal offices or the police station.

Sagunto
Ruins and Museum
Open: 10am-2pm and 4-6pm. Sunday 10am-2pm. Closed Monday and on holiday afternoons, also 1 January, Thursday and Friday in Holy Week and Christmas Day.

Valencia
Botanical Gardens
Calle Beato Gaspar Bono
Open: 10.30am-7.15pm.
☎ 331 16 57
Museum in the gardens
Open: 10am-2pm. Closed Monday, Wednesday, Friday and Sunday and on holidays.
☎ 331 06 06

Cathedral Museum
Open: 10am-1pm and 4-6pm. Closed in the afternoon on holidays and in December, January and February. ☎ 331 81 27

El Patriarca Collegiate Church
Plaza del Patriarca
Open: daily in summer. 11am-1.30pm Saturday and Sunday.
☎ 351 41 76

Ethnological Museum
Calle Corona 36
Open: 10am-1.30pm and 4-7pm.
10am-1.30pm and 4-9pm on
holidays.
☎ 331 90 70

Fallas Museum
Plaza Monteolivete
Open: 10am-2pm and 4-7pm.
Closed Monday.
☎ 332 33 36

Jardines del Real and Zoo
Calle San Pío V
Open: 10am until sunset.
☎ 369 19 44

Lonja de la Seda
Plaza del Mercado
Open: 11am-2pm and 4-6pm.
10am-2pm at weekends. Closed
Monday.

Municipal History Museum
In the City Hall
Open: 9am-2pm. Closed Saturday,
Sunday and holidays.
☎ 352 54 78

Museo de Bellas Artes
(Fine Arts Museum)
San Pio V, 9
Open: 10am-2pm and 4-6pm.
Closed on Sunday, Monday and
holiday afternoons during July,
August and September.
☎ 360 57 93

Museu de Prehistoria
Calle Corona 36
Open: 10am-1.30pm and 4-6pm.
Closed Monday and holiday
afternoons.
☎ 331 99 39

National Ceramics Museum
In the Dos Aguas Palace near the
Calle de la Paz
Open: 10am-2pm and 4-6pm.

Closed Sunday, Monday and on
holiday afternoons.
☎ 351 63 92

Taurino Museum
At the bullring
Open: 11am-1pm. Closed Saturday
and Sunday.
☎ 351 18 50

Torres de Serranos
Joaquín Saludes Maritime Museum
Open: 10am-1pm and 4-6.30pm
Tuesday to Friday.
☎ 331 90 70

Vila-real
Parish church
Sacristy open during services.

Villafamés
Museum of Contemporary Art
In the palace
Open: 11am-1pm and·3-7pm.
Remains open until 8pm in July,
August and September.

Information Offices

Benicarlo
Plaza San Andrés
☎ 964 47 31 80

Burriana
José Iturbi 33
☎ 964 51 15 40

Castellón de la Plana
Plaza de María Agustina 5
☎ 964 22 77 03

Cullera
Carrer del Riu 56
☎ 96 152 09 74

Gandia
Marqués de Campo, opposite the
station
☎ 96 287 45 44

or Paseo Marítimo Neptuno
☎ 96 284 24 07

Játiva
In the town hall
(No telephone number)

Oropesa
Av. de la Plana
☎ 964 31 00 20

Peñiscola
Paseo Marítimo
☎ 964 48 02 08

Sagunto
La Autonomia 2
☎ 96 246 12 30

Valencia
Plaza del Pais Valenciano
☎ 96 351 04 17
or Airport
☎ 96 153 03 25
or Cataluña 1
☎ 96 369 79 32

6

COSTA BLANCA

This famous stretch of coast corresponds exactly to Alicante, the province which fits neatly in between Valencia and Murcia, shaped like a crescent moon looking out across the Mediterranean. The shoreline, measuring just over 200km (124 miles), is made up of long, sandy beaches interrupted by rocky promontories or cliffs pitted with natural caves. The most mountainous region lies to the north and west, liberally sprinkled with atmospheric hill villages, ancient castles and small agricultural communities that have a timeless air about them. In the south an extensive plain, divided up more or less equally between sand and salt patches, has its own collection of lagoons, large number of date palms, introduced originally by Phoenicians and the Moors, and a pleasant selection of tourist attractions without too many high rise hotels and apartment blocks.

Historically the 'White Coast' differs in very few respects from any of its immediate neighbours. It was settled by the Iberians, the Phoenicians and the Greeks, appropriated by the Romans and the Visigoths, enriched by the Moors and recaptured by the Christians in the thirteenth century. When the Moriscos — Muslims who had been converted to Christianity — were expelled with some difficulty 300 years later, they took their agricultural expertise with them, leaving their orchards and farmlands to deteriorate alarmingly. These local Arabs were accused at the time of collaborating with the Berbers who made periodical sorties along the coast. However, this seems most unlikely because the pirate attacks continued in exactly the same way as before until the end of the seventeenth century.

The region managed to escape the worst traumas of the War of Succession and even the Civil War, while taking full advantage of any useful developments that came its way. In 1954 the province, which until then had very few hotels and *hostales*, made its bid for a share of the rapidly growing tourist industry and 11 years later was playing host to over a million holidaymakers from all over Europe. Nowadays more than twice that number fly into Alicante's El Altet airport, 20km (12 miles) from the capital. Many head straight for the fleshpots of Benidorm with its immense beaches and apparently inexhaustible supply of light entertainments, leaving the remainder to enjoy the other, less frenetic coastal resorts. Very few visitors venture inland apart from those who join a brief conducted tour, thereby leaving plenty of opportunities for travellers who prefer their own company.

The main route from Valencia, paralleled by the motorway for anyone in a hurry, bypasses the Cabo de San Antonio peninsula altogether. This means that it misses several places of interest with a good deal to offer on the way. For anyone with time to spare, a coast road branches off to the left just across the border and follows the sea down to **Denia**, which was founded by the Greeks from Asia Minor and known to the Romans as *Dianium* in honour of their goddess Diana. The old fortress occupying a hill above the town resists any temptation to claim a close association with the Moors, although the region was once part of Al-Andalus with responsibilities for the Balearic Islands and Sardinia. It makes an ideal setting for the Moros y Cristianos during the San Roque festival in August when ancient encounters between the inhabitants and the Berber pirates are re-enacted with colourful costumes and boundless enthusiasm. This follows the Santisima Sangre fiesta in early July, dating back to 1624 and marked by theatres and concerts, floral battles, fireworks and the unusual *bous en la mar*. This literally means 'bullfighting in the sea' but is actually a novel version of bull running through the streets. It ends in a temporary semi-circular ring on the beach outside the harbour, when no attempt is made to kill the bull.

Denia has one or two other interesting historical places such as the seventeenth-century church of Santa María and the Archaeological Museum. There are a handful of hotels, a wide selection of restaurants and eight different campsites, some of which are open all year. At one time Denia was famous for its muscatel grapes but nowadays it relies on fishing, citrus fruit and holidaymakers, including all the families who have second homes in the vicinity. A ferry also keeps the port in daily touch with the island of Ibiza. The beaches are pleasantly sandy on the northern shore but rocky to the south with delightfully isolated little coves overlooked by an old watchtower

COSTA BLANCA

known as the Torre del Gerro.

About 10km (6 miles) south of Denia, on the far side of the Cabo de San Antonia, **Jávea** has ample facilities for tourists. The beaches are rather small by comparison but there are numerous grottoes like the Cave of Skulls and the Cova Tallada with its little freshwater lake and eye-catching stalactites. Some of these caves can only be reached by boat although there are some ladders down the cliff face where the dangerous conditions have led some people to call them the *pesqueras de la muerte* (fishing grounds of death).

Care must also be taken by anyone sailing along the coast because of the jagged rocks lying just below the surface which are very

Opposite:Windsurf boards can be hired on the beach at Calpe (top);
A souvenir shop in Gata de Gorgos selling wicker baskets (bottom)

popular with divers and underwater fishermen. Jávea is a pleasing mixture of the old and the new. Its ancient district clusters round a fortified Gothic church while its modern counterparts consist of housing developments augmented by shops, a pleasure boat harbour, a nine hole golf course, three campsites, hotels and a *parador*.

It is a pleasing, though short, rural drive down to the Playa de la Granadella, a happy hunting ground for underwater swimmers and open-air enthusiasts. Meanwhile, a secondary road cuts across country to **Moraira**, an ancient fishing port presided over by its own antiquated tower and matching castle. Although it boasts one comfortable hotel, other less ambitious establishments, villas, a variety of shops and a few restaurants, it is still something of a backwater as far as tourists go. It is within easy reach of two different golf courses and shares a selection of campsites with Tuelada and Benisa, a short distance away on the inland highway to Calpe.

Anyone driving down from Valencia who prefers to follow the main road to Calpe rather than meander round the coast would save enough time to visit the safari park at **Vergel**. It covers a large area with spacious enclosures where animals such as lions and tigers can be seen, separated from each other by strong gates manned by rangers. The animals take little notice of motorists who are, nevertheless, instructed to stay in their cars and keep all the windows closed. No such rules apply in other sections of the park where visitors can wander across the grass surrounded by buck and zebra, llamas and deer, as well as an occasional Shetland pony. There are elephants and camels; giraffe share their compounds quite happily with ostriches, not far from an extremely vocal colony of monkeys; while dolphins entertain the crowds surrounding their large pool. There is a restaurant where you can get a grilled meal or a snack either indoors or outside on the terrace under the trees.

Beyond Vergel the main road squeezes its way through **Gata de Gorgos** where the streets are lined with little shops selling useful articles and souvenirs. It is a good place to buy leather goods, wickerwork, a beach mat or a mock sombrero. Gata is about half way to **Calpe** with its famous Peñón de Ifach, a massive rock that bears a striking resemblance to Gibraltar and is also joined to the mainland by a narrow strip rather like a giant causeway. A busy holiday resort, complete with highrise blocks, hotels, gardens and promenades has grown up beside the beaches on either side, almost obliterating all traces of the Greeks, the Romans and the Moors who once lived there. A tunnel has been bored up through the rock to the summit more than 320m (1,050ft) above sea level, with its gulls' eye view of the coast down to Altea. Anyone who is fond of lobsters should stop at **Altea** for lunch or even spend the night at one of its oldest but quite well equipped hotels. It is essentially a fishing port with a boating club, a sports harbour, sandy beaches and attractive little coves and an esplanade lined with open-air bars and restaurants. The old part of the town rises steeply up the hillside with a number of alleys that are more like stairways and a blue-domed parish church right at the top. There are a handful of campsites in the vicinity and three more at **Alfaz del Pi** just down the road, two of which provide bungalows and stay open right through the year.

Visitors in search of something out of the ordinary will find an amazing garden hidden away behind a number of unexceptional villas on the right hand side of the road to San Rafael. It is known as the Museo Delso and is hard to find because there are only a few dilapidated signs pointing the way to it. However, it is easily identified by the two large yellow eggs on a wall beside the equally unusual wrought iron gates. Lining the drive are strange sculptures and lamp posts resembling railway signals, a barbecue shaped like a primitive totem head has a gaping mouth for the fireplace while frying pans and pokers are suspended like earrings from the lobes on either side. There are likenesses of President De Gaulle and Napoleon, two windmills serving as folk museums are dedicated to Don Quixote and Sancho Panza, and a realistic witch guards an open grotto. The whole extraordinary set-up is the brain child of Pedro Delso, an artist and sculptor who ran away to South America when he was 12. He met Picasso in Paris, claims he took Cubism a step further by inventing triangulism, and soon became famous with examples of his work on show all the way from Scandinavia to Mexico via a North Sea oil rig and the underground stations in Barcelona. He and his wife are planning to open the Museo Delso to the public at regular intervals but in the meantime visitors are seldom turned away, even though they arrive by the coachload every week and frequently leave with a memento bought in the gallery at the bottom of the hill.

Benidorm, the highrise, concrete and glass coastal resort spread out along 7km (4 miles) of sandy beaches, is a firm favourite with more than 2 million holidaymakers who converge on it every year. It is modern and extremely lively, crammed with every possible attraction from pelota matches, where spectators can bet on the results, to glittering extravaganzas produced on what is claimed to be the biggest stage in the world. Sporting activities include tennis, riding, bowling and mountain climbing as well as sailing, windsurfing, diving and fishing. It has hotels of every size and description, a wide range of bars and restaurants, plenty of furnished accommodation and space for 5,000 people in its local campsites.

Benidorm was invaded by successive armies, although its only reminders of the past are a few old streets where the fishermen and farmers lived less than 50 years ago. Spaniards living up in the mountains were the first to recognise its potential as a holiday resort. They were followed by the Germans who were joined shortly afterwards by the English and the Scandinavians. Development started in earnest during the 1950s and today Benidorm is one of the best known and most crowded all-the-year-round holiday playgrounds on the Mediterranean.

With so little to offer in the way of historical associations, Benidorm has made a point of building the occasional castle and enveloping the inshore island of Plumbaria in myths and legends. The island makes a pleasant outing from the mainland with boat services running about once an hour in full view of the star-shaped observation platform known as El Castillo. Meanwhile, guests who book in for dinner at the Gran Castillo Conde de Alfaz are invited to wear crowns and watch medieval jousting in the banqueting hall, augmented by an invasion from outer space. By way of contrast, a Mexican-style ranch combines open-air barbecues with Latin American music followed by a disco in a ballroom decked with flags.

There are several places of interest within easy reach of Benidorm. An attractive road winds its way through orchards and pinewoods to Polop, a picturesque hamlet. It then heads on to **Callosa d'En Sarrià** (sometimes written Callosa de Ensarrià), the centre of an agricultural area which still uses many of the farming practices introduced by the Moors. The village of Callosa was bought from the king in 1290 by Admiral Bernat de Sarrià who promptly added his name to it, an exercise in personal publicity that was officially confirmed in 1985. The writer Jaume Roig took refuge in the castle some 200 years later to avoid an epidemic in Valencia and the book he wrote there has outlived the fortifications with the exception of two gates, the Portal del Carrer Major and the Portal de Bolulla. Other reminders of the past include a much restored fourteenth-century church, an elderly convent and El Puador, a spring in the ancient quarter that was originally used for washing clothes.

The town is noted for its markets where things like clothes, ceramics and confectionery are sold on Mondays, fruit, flowers and vegetables on Tuesdays and Saturdays. Callosa d'En Sarrià takes as much pride in its local dishes as it does in the two main fiestas, the

Benidorm — plenty of sun, sea and crowds

A lacemaker in Guadalest

first in honour of San Jaume in late July which centres round traditional dancing in the Plaza de España. The celebrations marking the
feast of Our Lady of Injurias on the second Sunday in October are
rather more elaborate, devoted to the reconstruction of ancient
battles between the Moors and the Christians. Nearby at El Algar —
a tourist site on the river at the entrance to the valley — donkeys are
available for a short trip up to the source, officially described as the
Fuentes de Algar but actually some attractive waterfalls.

From Callosa d'En Sarrià the road to Alcoy calls in at **Guadalest**
where the mountains are more impressive and the terrain becomes
increasingly arid, better suited to almonds and olives than market
gardens. Guadalest is full of souvenirs, beginning with a modern
ceramics emporium festooned with pots and plates, jars, mirrors,
stylised hay forks and various odds and ends. Beyond it is the
amazing Castell de Guadalest, an ancient village enclosed in a ruined
fortress whose only entrance is through an arched doorway set in a
crevasse between tall limestone peaks. There is nothing to see from
the road except for one or two cottages, souvenirs and empty coaches
parked in rows. Unfortunately the site is more noteworthy than the
village because this was largely destroyed by an earthquake in 1744,
leaving only a few buildings still standing. However, there are
excellent views from the Castillo San José down to the sea in one
direction and across the reservoir to the mountains further inland. A
small road, better suited to jeeps than cars, circles round the lake to
rejoin the main route a few kilometres further on.

An alternative and, at times, rather tortuous route back to the coast
is the A170 through Sella with an early deviation to Penáguila, where
there is a ruined castle as well as some old houses, the Garden of
Santos and a safari park. **Sella** itself is a picturesque huddle of
whitewashed buildings on the lower slopes of Santa Barbara, a large
bare mountain that looms over it. In Moorish times the village was
known as *Tagarinos*, a name which lingers on in the Tagarina gorges
where it is said that a splendid treasure trove was discovered in the
early nineteenth century. A feudal palace and a medieval tower are
the most obvious landmarks while its favourite pastimes are hunting, mainly for partridges and rabbits, and two traditional ball
games called *galocha* and *de llargues*. From Sella a less demanding,
although still minor road skirts round the Amadorio reservoir,
crosses over the motorway and reaches the outskirts of Villajoyosa.
However, it is also possible to take a longer way round through
Finestrat whose roots are firmly planted in prehistoric times.

The village, perched on the ridge of a limestone outcrop, appears to have been occupied in the fourth century BC but there are no traces of the Romans who were succeeded by Syrian troops from Balch during the Moorish takeover. The Muslims preferred to set up their own communities rather than move into Christian settlements which they regarded as impure, so Finestrat suited them perfectly. They built a fortress which was demolished in the 1920s to provide building materials for the hermitage of Santo Cristo del Remedio, but there are a few sparse remains of the Alcasser where the mayor used to live. Their ancient farming practices can still be seen all the way down to a strip along the foreshore near **Villajoyosa**. This is a colourful little port where tourists are beginning to outnumber the local inhabitants at the height of the season. Its attractions include a comfortable hotel, furnished apartments, campsites, a pleasure boat harbour and a steadily increasing number of restaurants. There are plenty of sports facilities, with opportunities for tennis and several other ball games as well as fishing and windsurfing. There is also a modern casino that stays open until 4am.

South of Villajoyosa the highway and the *autopista* follow the seashore before the N340 heads for the interior. The first town of any consequence along this route is **Jijona** which, according to the townspeople, is one of the most affluent communities in the country. It is a delightful little place which owes its undoubted prosperity to *turron*, a sweetmeat introduced by the Arabs, mentioned in *The Thousand and One Nights* and now an essential part of Christmas all over the country. According to the dictionary of the Royal Spanish Academy, it is made of almonds, pine nuts, hazelnuts or walnuts, all toasted and mixed with honey, although there are some variations that call for egg yolk, sugar and even chocolate. The countryside around Jijona is largely devoted to bees and almonds and supplies the local factories with a large percentage of their ingredients.

One factory, the Turrones El Lobo y 1880, on the outskirts of the town, has a small but interesting museum. It contains original equipment used in the production of *turron* and also a few traditional costumes worn by the wealthy landowners as well as those of factory workers and farm labourers. Thirteen kilometres (8 miles) from Jijona are the Caves of Canalobre, 700m (2,300ft) up in the Cabescó d'Or mountains near the village of Busot. They are full of splendid stalactites and stalagmites, extravagantly illuminated and best seen from a steep but quite manageable stairway built along the inner rock formations. Back in the open air there is a concert hall, a bar with a large terrace and extensive views down to the Mediterranean.

Beyond Jijona the N340 presses on through the mountains to

Alcoy, known with considerable justification as the City of Bridges, one of which is reminiscent of the New Bridge at Ronda, in Andalucia. Although Alcoy was inhabited by the Iberians, the Romans and the Arabs, all of whom left traces of their passing, the present city only dates back to 1255. Jaume I decided that he needed an outpost on the road from Valencia to Murcia and chose the point at which the existing route had to negotiate a series of deep gullies where the Molinar and Riquer rivers met to form the Río Serpis. As soon as the town became firmly established the Moors wanted it back, the defenders appealed to St George for help and he materialised over the battlements, thereby ensuring a Christian victory. The event is celebrated in April every year when the two splendidly dressed armies fight for possession of a wooden castle in the Plaza de España with a young boy playing the part of St George. The centre of the medieval city was the Placeta del Carbó, now partly occupied by the Camilo Visedo, or Municipal Museum of Archaeology. It is full of historical relics, the most important of which is the Plom d'Alcoi, a tablet made of lead, carved in Ancient Greek but incorporating an Iberian alphabet.

When the people of Alcoy found that the city needed more room, but could not expand sideways because of the mountains, they demolished all the old one-storey houses and replaced them with highrise apartment blocks and offices. However, one old mansion was reprieved and is now the headquarters of the Associació de Sant Jordi which is responsible for all the local festivals and keeps paraphernalia associated with them in its crowded Museo de Fiestas del Casal de Sant Jordi. The town was largely taken over by industry towards the end of the eighteenth century after which it was the scene of social upheaval when factories were destroyed, resulting in unemployment which led to further unrest. However, Alcoy continued to prosper, new bridges were built and wealthy newcomers introduced Modernist buildings, especially in the Carrer San Nicolás. Today it continues to bustle, producing paper, making machinery and canning olives, often stuffed with anchovies.

The countryside around Alcoy is well known for its trees (especially oaks), the profusion and variety of its medicinal plants and herbs like mint, thyme and rosemary, a scattering of prehistoric caves and several small hermitages. At one of these, dedicated to the Virgen de los Lirios, visitors are encouraged to dip their hands in the

Opposite: Inside the Caves of Canalobre (top);
colourful tiles adorn this house in Biar (bottom)

fountain to see how long they can stand the ice cold temperature of the water. Many of the surrounding villages, like Barxell and Bañeres, have their own tangible reminders from the distant past but the trio of castles at Biar, Sax and Villena are by far the most impressive. The best way of reaching them is along the A210, which branches off the route from Alcoy to Jijona, looks in at Ibi where more toys are produced than anywhere else in Spain, and carries on without further interruption to **Biar**. This is a picturesque hamlet, completely overshadowed by its large, well preserved Arab fortress, dominated in turn by a twelfth-century keep. The ancient quarter clusters on the hillside below the castle walls in a medley of steep cobbled streets, winding alleys, little squares, old fountains and brilliantly coloured potted plants. Among its inbuilt defences are a series of archways that could be closed off during the Middle Ages to provide greater security at night or discourage invaders in the event of a surprise attack. The church of Our Lady of the Assumption, thought to have been built on the site of an ancient mosque, was completed in 1519 but unfortunately the Renaissance façade is showing considerable signs of wear and tear.

Villena, 7km (4 miles) to the west, is a good deal larger than Biar, having been an important stronghold in the Middle Ages with control over many of the nearby castles and owing allegiance to the kingdom of Castile. The castle of La Atalaya is a splendid example of medieval military architecture, solid and rather severe but relieved to a certain extent by a number of sentry boxes, added like a series of jam jars to the top of the keep in the fifteenth century. Among its various owners was Henry of Aragon who wrote poetry and was also a magician. The church of Santiago, with its attractive spiral columns, is older than the church of Santa María by about 100 years and makes an excellent foil for the town hall which also faces onto the square. Part of the building is occupied by the Archaeological Museum, worth visiting for its collection of gold and silver Iberian treasures and several examples of early ceramic work. The Festero Museum is only open during the September celebrations, when its costumes are needed for the feast of its patron saint.

Some 10km (6 miles) to the south the N330 skirts round the equally ancient village of **Sax** whose fortress is balanced even more dramatically on the highest point of a jagged limestone spur. There is a Museum of the Moors and Christians in the fortress. From here anyone in search of more remnants from the past will find an antiquated castle at Petrel and the blue-domed hermitage of Santa Barbara in Monovar, an industrious little community off the main road whose factories turn out leather, wax candles, soap, wicker-work and shoes. On the far side of La Mola castle, an Arab fortress that has been extensively restored, and the much more modern Sanctuary of La Magdalena, built in the Gothic style, motorists are faced with a choice of routes. The left hand fork makes straight for Alicante on the coast, leaving its counterpart to provide a shortcut to Crevillente on the main road to Murcia.

Anyone interested in Modernist architecture would undoubtedly enjoy the museum in **Novelda**, particularly as it is easily accessible from either road. Gaudí and his contemporaries had a tremendous influence on the town and the house with its red brick, limestone and ornamental grilles would not look out of place in Barcelona. The interior is light and spacious with everything from the wallpaper to the door handles designed especially to blend in with their sur-roundings. It has been furnished in the same style and claims to be unusual, if not unique, on the Costa Blanca.

Although **Alicante** is both the provincial capital and the gateway to the Costa Blanca for the endless batallions of holidaymakers who fly in every year, it has succeeded in retaining a typically Spanish atmosphere, capable of absorbing its visitors rather than being overwhelmed by them. There are regular train services to several other large cities including Madrid and Barcelona, coaches run at frequent intervals to places as far afield as Granada, Almería, Jaén and Málaga, leaving fleets of buses to keep in contact with many leading coastal resorts. The city has plenty of hotels, a wide range of cafés and restaurants, furnished apartments and campsites.

As for beaches, there are superb stretches of sand on either side, notably at San Juan which is very built up and extremely busy during the summer months. It is also well supplied with hotels, *hostales*, apartments, restaurants and bars as well as discos, an open-air cinema and a good choice of shops. The facilities for water sports enthusiasts include pedaloes and windsurfing equipment for hire while anyone without a car who wants a complete change of scenery can travel up to Denia and back on a narrow-gauge railway. The Playa Postiguet, near the port at the end of the esplanade, is some-what less attractive but every bit as crowded at the height of the season. There are opportunities for fishing and picnicking near El Palmeral, a park on the route to the south, while the Saladar beach at Agua Amarga, 6km (4 miles) away, has villas, shops, restaurants and bars all along the promenade. Nearby is a nudist zone, easily accessible from both the beach and the main coast road to the airport.

Alicante can trace its history back to the Greeks who called it *Akra*

Alicante's busy harbour provides shelter for both pleasure boats and local fishing boats

Alicante's market has an abundance of locally grown, fresh produce

This superb carving adorns the exterior of Alicante's cathedral

Alicante has many interesting buildings

Leuka, which the Romans promptly translated as *Lucentum*, the 'City of Light'. Its oldest and most impressive building is the Castillo de Santa Barbara, said to have been started by the Carthaginians in the third century BC and constantly rebuilt, enlarged, improved and adapted to meet the requirements of its successive occupants. It was captured by the Moors in the eighth century, played a major role in the disputes between Aragon and Castile 500 years later, was garrisoned by the English, and blown up by Philip V during the Spanish War of Succession. It is still a splendid fortress high up on Mount Benacantil, with moats and drawbridges, tunnels, guardrooms and dungeons and the ruins of what was once the governor's palace. There is a lift up from the Paseo de Gomis near the beach as well as a footpath that starts close to the church of Santa María on the Plaza del Puente, in the old quarter below the castle walls. The church, built about 700 years ago on the site of an ancient mosque, has an ornate Baroque façade added in the eighteenth century, a somewhat overdecorated sanctuary and a large, eye-catching marble font. One of its nearest neighbours is La Asegurada, the oldest mansion in the city and now the Museum of Contemporary Art. Its extensive collection of paintings and sculptures, donated for the most part by Eusebio Sempere, includes works by Joan Miró, Dali and Picasso.

A few blocks away, the palatial town hall with its matching towers, blue-tiled dome and understated stone carvings has a very unusual feature. On the steps leading up to it there is a spot which is used to calculate the exact height above sea level of any other place in Spain. The interior's attractions include a modest collection of paintings, fairly ornate salons and a much decorated chapel. The nearby cathedral of San Nicolás de Bari, built in the early seventeenth century, was badly damaged during the Civil War but managed to preserve its altarpieces and the Renaissance cloister which pre-dates the church by about 200 years. However, the Monasterio de la Santa Faz goes one better as far as relics are concerned, having been built to house yet another piece of the veil which St Veronica is said to have used to wipe the face of Christ on the road to Calvary. A pilgrimage to Santa Faz takes place on the Thursday after Easter when a crowd of up to 100,000 people makes its way to the monastery, stopping en route for liqueur-flavoured buns and glasses of sweet white wine. Having paid their respects to the ancient relic in its silver casket, most of the pilgrims buy a souvenir or two before finding a spot under the trees for a picnic lunch.

Alicante holds its own version of the Fallas, similar to the celebrations in Valencia, from 21 to 24 June accompanied by parades, competitions, sporting events, bullfights and firework displays, culminating in the *crema* when all but one of the fallas go up in flames. The next morning merrymaking breaks out afresh in honour of St Peter and continues unabated for another 5 days. Concerts, theatre performances and ballet mark the feast of Our Lady of Remedies, the perpetual Mayoress of Alicante, in early August when the statue of the Virgin is escorted from the cathedral and carried in solemn procession through the crowded streets. After this there is a breathing space before fresh supplies of gunpowder are handed round for the Moors and the Christians to 'fight' for possession of the city on the anniversary of its liberation in December nearly 750 years ago. Other memorable occasions include Carnival, Holy Week and the Easter Sunday picnics when many people arm themselves with a *mona*, a type of roll with a boiled egg in the middle, to be broken over the head of anyone the owner finds attractive. It causes so much hilarity that it is often repeated on Easter Monday.

The Explanada de España in Alicante is particularly attractive, its walkway patterned in wavy lines of cream, red and black marble and shaded by tall palm trees, overlooking the pleasure boats tucked away in one corner of the harbour. From here a ferry service is available to the offshore island of Tabarca, about 1 hour away. The name dates back to the sixteenth century when several hundred Italians from Genoa, who had been captured by the Berbers and held prisoner on the Tunisian island of Tabarca, were rescued and given a temporary home there. Apart from a number of fishermen's cottages, the Casa del Gobernador and the tower of San José, its main attractions are the translucent water, submerged reefs, rocky inlets and little caves such as the Grotto of the Sea Wolf, so called because one of these creatures is said to have been discovered there many years ago. It is a favourite spot with divers, underwater fishermen and swimmers as well as tourists on a day trip from the mainland. There are no hotels on the island but plenty of outdoor restaurants specialising in such traditional dishes as seafood paella and *arroz negro*, or black rice, which is made with squid whose ink is one of the principal ingredients.

Along the coast is **Santa Pola**, an important fishing port with plenty for tourists and ferries to Tabarca that take about 30 minutes. It has a selection of quite modern hotels with lifts and private bathrooms, some furnished accommodation and two campsites that are open throughout the year. The beach is wide and sandy with facilities for all types of water sports in addition to tennis courts, a large swimming pool, a boating club and moorings for pleasure craft. The fishing fleet, one of the largest on the coast, not only supplies all the cafés and restaurants with everything from crabs to sole and lobsters, but also attracts a good many buyers and sightseers at sundown when the day's catch is put up for auction on the quay near the harbour entrance. A fortress occupying one side of the Plaza Castillo is the only building that could really be described as historic but the town makes up for this with a colourful procession in honour of the Virgen del Carmen in mid July and a week-long fiesta dedicated to its patron saint at the beginning of September.

Santa Pola also has the undoubted advantage of being a mere 14km (9 miles) from **Elche**, one of the great showplaces of the Costa Blanca. It is famous for having the only date-palm groves in Europe, laid out by the Phoenicians more than 2,000 years ago, to which it has added quite a few other attractions such as the famous Dama de Elche, discovered in 1897. She is a haughty-looking Iberian beauty, with a magnificent head-dress and much jewellery, who is considered to be one of the most outstanding exhibits of her time on display in the National Museum of Archaeology in Madrid. Several replicas of the Dame can be seen in Elche, one of them presiding over a limpid pool in the Huerto del Cura, or Priest's Orchard, on the Calle Federico Garcia Sanchiz. This is an exotic garden full of cacti, bougainvillea and other plants including a remarkable palm tree, known as the Palmera Imperial, which has seven trunks growing out of a single root and is thought to be more than 150 years old. Foremost among the other gardens is the Parque Municipal, where there is a small museum, rivalled by the Parque Deportivo next door, devoted mainly to swimming and other outdoor activities.

Elche has about 200,000 date palms, collectively titled El Palmeral, which supplied the Moors with all the fruit they needed. Although very little is harvested these days, large quantities of fronds are removed every year and distributed throughout the country in time for the Palm Sunday celebrations. Other sources of revenue are agriculture, shoe manufacture and the tourist industry. There are few hotels in the town apart from one comfortable establishment described as a *parador colaborador* and located across the road from the Huerto del Cura. However, there are plenty of restaurants and five campsites, one of them surrounded by date palms and another conveniently situated on the Carretera de Circunvalacion Sur near the turning off to El Pinet on the coast below Santa Pola.

Sightseeing in Elche is delightfully simple because all the main attractions are grouped together within a few blocks of each other, except for the Museum of Contemporary Art in the old Moorish quarter of El Ravall de Sant Joan. A good starting point might well be the town hall, dating in part from the fifteenth century with a distinctive clock tower that was added 200 years later. A short walk away, further up the river, are the hermitage of San Sebastián, the Alcázar de la Señora, which changed its name to the Palacio de Altamira and houses the Archaeological Museum, and the Arab fortress of La Calahorra. The famous basilica of Santa María is an impressive building in its own right which replaced an ancient mosque but had to be completely restored after a flash flood in 1672. This was a blessing in disguise because it enabled the powers-that-be to make some improvements they considered necessary for staging the incredible Misterio de Elche, Europe's oldest mystery play, performed on 15 August for more than 600 years.

Elche was finally recaptured from the Moors in 1266 and found to have a small Christian community with an exceptional devotion to the Virgin Mary. Alfonso the Wise immediately sent them a long narrative verse about the Assumption and this formed the basis of a play, set entirely to music which turned it into a Byzantine grand opera. The performance has not altered and even the methods used for the most spectacular sequences are exactly the same as those employed in the late fifteenth century. So many people are anxious to join the congregation that condensed versions of the Mystery of Elche are staged on three separate days before the main event and again on All Saints Day (1 November).

La Alcudia, about 2km (1 mile) from Elche on the road to Dolores, is the site of *Illici*, the old Roman settlement previously occupied by the Iberians, where the Dama de Elche was discovered. There is little to see apart from some ancient columns, excavated foundations and a large well, all surrounded by fields of globe artichokes and a few date palms. However, a number of the items that came to light are on display in a small museum near the entrance to the site. From here it is hardly worth looking for a shortcut because the Elche ring road joins the N340 on the outskirts of the town. The only reason for stopping in Crevillente is to see a number of floats used in the Easter Week processions that are kept in the Mariano Benlliure Museum in the crypt of the church of Nuestra Señora de Belén.

Twenty-two kilometres (14 miles) down the road, **Orihuela**, a pleasant town on the banks of the Río Segura, was the capital of Murcia under both the Visigoths and the Arabs but is now in Alicante, just short of the border. It has its own palm grove but shows considerably more interest in the citrus orchards that have been laid out all round. The most impressive of all its ancient buildings is El

Salvador cathedral, built in the fourteenth century and memorable chiefly for its spiral pillars, highly original vaulting and the Cathedral Museum of Sacred Art. This contains a number of fine paintings including *The Temptation of St Thomas Aquinas* by Velázquez.

The University of Orihuela was founded in the sixteenth century in what is now the College of Santo Domingo, but was closed down after about 200 years. The building has two separate cloisters, one of which was badly damaged during the Civil War, and a large church full of frescoes and with some exuberant stucco mouldings in the chancel. The church of Santiago is somewhat older, having been founded by the Catholic Monarchs, and has some very viewable statues as well as a number of items that belonged to the Knights of Santiago, lodged for safekeeping in the treasury. Apart from a couple of quite interesting little churches and old mansions like the Rubalcava Palace, the city is known principally for its Gregorian music and the sound of bells. Its most outstanding celebration is the Fiesta de la Reconquista in mid-July when two lights are placed in the castle ruins as a tribute to San Justa and San Rufina who apparently led the Christian army through a weak spot in the defences and so enabled them to recapture the whole area from the Moors.

Orihuela has little to offer in the way of hotels, traditional restaurants or convenient campsites, preferring to leave that side of things to the nearby coastal resorts of **Guardamar del Segura** and Torrevieja. The former, some 30km (20 miles) away, is thought to have provided the early Greek traders with large quantities of salt before the Romans took over the port. They were followed by the Moors who lost it to Ferdinand in the thirteenth century, after which it was battered quite regularly until the town was eventually destroyed by an earthquake in 1829. Among its few remnants from the past are traces of an Iberian cemetery in the Cabezo del Lucero on the way to Rojales, a ruined castle and a memorial stone. It proclaims that the mosque to which it was attached was built 'in the name of Allah in the month of Moharen in the year 333' and gives a lot of other details. Unfortunately, the building no longer exists. Today Guardamar is an up-and-coming holiday playground with long smooth beaches, backed by sand dunes covered in pines, eucalyptus and palms. There are a handful of hotels in addition to several *hostales* and seaside boarding houses, as well as restaurants specialising in seafood like prawns and baby eels. The town's campsites can accommodate about 2,000 people at almost any time of the year. The most popular local sports include both indoor and outdoor football, tennis, swimming, basketball and cycling.

To the south of Guardamar del Segura are the Laguna Salada de la Mata and the Laguna Salada de Torrevieja, two enormous salt lagoons which, between them, produce well over 1 million tons a year. The salt is allowed to crystallise before being piled up in a series of sparkling white hillocks along the water's edge and it is possible to call in and see exactly how it is made.

The town of **Torrevieja**, the last place of any size on the Costa Blanca, is fairly modern, having been completely destroyed in the earthquake of 1829. New buildings are still going up all along the waterfront to provide additional hotels and furnished apartments. In addition to these, there are two campsites, as well as houses and bungalows spread over quite a wide area. A reconstructed Arab watchtower stands guard on the top of a nearby cliff but it is the only place of any interest to would-be sightseers. However, the list of sports facilities includes the Club de Golf Villamartin, a pleasant eighteen hole course within easy reach along the main highway to the south, followed by a short approach road that turns off at La Zenia. The Aquapark has all the usual attractions apart from a restaurant so visitors are advised to take their own picnics but are warned that tins, bottles and animals must be left at home. The resort also has an aero-club, tennis courts and football grounds, a bullring, moorings available from the Club Nautico and a whole host of minute satellite *playas* overlooking the Mediterranean all the way down to the border with Murcia.

Additional Information

Places of Interest

Alcoy
Archaeological Museum
San Miguel 29
Open: 8am-1.30pm and 5.30-8pm.
Closed holidays.
☎ 965 54 03 02

Museo de Fiestas del Casal de Sant Jordi
San Miguel 60
Open: 10am-1.30pm and 5.30-8pm on weekdays. 10am-1.30pm Saturday and holidays.
☎ 965 34 29 61

Alfaz del Pi
Museo Delso
Off the road to San Rafael
No set opening hours at the moment but enquire at any reasonable time.

Alicante
Archaeological Museum
Palacio de la Diputación
General Mola 6
Open: 9am-2pm on weekdays. 11am-1pm on holidays. Closed Monday.
☎ 965 12 13 00 or 965 22 13 02

Castillo de Santa Barbara
Open: 9am-9pm June to September.
9am-8pm April and May. 9am-7pm
October to March. Closed Saturday
afternoon.

Cathedral
Calle San Nicolas
Open: 10am-12.30pm and 6-8.30pm
on weekdays. 9am-1.45pm on
holidays.

Ferries to the Island of Tabarca
Times vary according to the
demand. Enquire at the Tourist
Office (see below for numbers).

La Asegurada
Museum of Contemporary Art
Plaza de Santa María
Open: 10.30am-1.30pm and 6-9pm.
Closed Sunday afternoon and
Monday May to September. 10am-
1pm and 5-8pm. Closed Monday
October to April.

Monasterio de la Santa Faz
Open: 11am-1pm and 5-8pm on
weekdays.

Town Hall
Plaza de Ayuntamiento
Open: 9am-3pm Monday to Friday.

Caves of Canalobre
Near Busot
Open: 10.30am-8.30pm April to
September. 11am-6.30pm October
to March. Closed 1 January and 25
December.

Crevillente
Mariano Benlliure Museum
In the church of Nuestra Señora de
Belén. Open: 11am-1.30pm and 5-
7.30pm. Closed Sunday and
Monday July to September and
11am-2pm on holidays.
☎ 965 40 05 34

Denia
Archaeological Museum
In the castle
Open: 10am-2pm and 5-8pm.
☎ 965 78 01 87

Elche
Archaeological Museum
In the Altamira Palace
Open: 11am-1pm and 4-7pm on
weekdays and holidays.
☎ 965 45 13 13

Huerto del Cura
Federico Garcia Sanchiz
Open: 9am-8pm in summer. 9am-
6pm mid-September to mid-June.

La Alcudia Museum
On the site outside Elche
Open: daily except Monday but
may sometimes close for lunch.

Jávea
Historic and Ethnological Museum
Open: Saturday afternoon and
Sunday morning.
☎ 965 79 01 98

Jijona
Turrones El Lobo y 1880
Factory and Turron Museum
Open: daily 9.30am-1pm and 4-
8pm.

Orihuela
Cathedral Museum of Sacred Art
Open: daily 10.30am-12.30pm.
Closed Sunday and holidays.
☎ 965 30 01 40

Church of Santiago
Open: 9am-1pm and 4-6pm.

La Granja Palace
Open: 11am-1pm and 4-7pm.
Closed Sunday and holidays.

Museum of the Reconquest
In the Rubalcava Palace
Open: 11am-1pm and 4-7pm.

Santo Domingo College
Ronda de Santo Domingo
Open: 9am-1pm and 4-6pm. Closed
Saturday, Sunday and holidays.

Penáguita
Aitana Safari Park
Open: 10am-6.30pm in summer.
10am-5pm in winter.

Sax
*Museum of the Moors and the
Christians*
In the castle
Open: 5-7pm on Saturday. 12noon-
2pm and 5-7pm Sunday and
holidays. Can be seen on request
during the week.
☎ 965 47 40 06

Vergel
Safari Park
Open: 10am-7.30pm in summer.
10am-6pm in winter.

Villena
Archaeological Museum
In the town hall
Plaza de Santiago
Open: all day during the week.
☎ 965 80 04 29 or 965 80 11 50

Information Offices

Alcoy
General Sanjurjo 3
☎ 34 32 84
or Av. Puente San Jorge 1
☎ 33 28 57

Alicante
Explanada de España 2
☎ 21 22 85
also Portugal 17
☎ 22 38 02

Altea
Paseo Marítimo
☎ 88 88 23

Benidorm
Martínez Alejos 16
☎ 85 32 24

Calpe
Av. Ejércitos Españoles 40
☎ 83 12 50

Denia
Patricio Ferrándiz
☎ 78 09 57

Elche
Parque Municipal
☎ 45 27 47

Javea
Plaza Almirante Bastarreche
☎ 79 07 36

Orihuela
Plaza Condesa Vía Manuel 1
☎ 30 02 96

Santa Pola
Plaza de la Diputación
☎ 41 49 84

Torrevieja
Av. de la Libertad 11
☎ 71 07 22

Villajoyosa
Plaza de la Inglesia
☎ 89 30 43

7

COSTA CALIDA

The Costa Cálida is the least known stretch of Mediterranean coastline in Spain. There are few cosy little seaside resorts and hardly any modern developments apart from La Manga on the Mar Menor. However, as the name means 'Warm Coast' it can only be a matter of time before the tranquillity of its small, out-of-the-way beaches is submerged under a wave of tourism. It has plenty of historic sites, varied scenery and ancient festivals as well as little spas, sports facilities and unexpected items such as the world's first electrically-powered submarine.

The province of Murcia, whose foreshore corresponds to the Costa Cálida, has four close neighbours, Alicante and Albacete to the north, and Granada and Almería on its border with Andalucía. Apart from the provincial capital and the ancient port of Cartagena, there are hardly any large towns to speak of but quite a number of sizeable communities as well as isolated hamlets which have changed very little down the centuries.

The countryside is arid and stony to the north but a system of canals, possibly introduced by the Romans but undoubtedly perfected by the Moors, has turned the plains into fertile agricultural land producing mainly grain, citrus fruit, grapes and vegetables. The coastline is fairly mountainous although it levels out into a series of dunes and sandbanks in the Mar Menor region. The population is very unevenly distributed as the majority of people live in the towns and villages, along the river courses, in the mining areas or on the coastal belt with the remainder scattered thinly over the hillsides, often with no means of access apart from country lanes or cart tracks. Each outlying homestead has its own well to provide drinking water, irrigate a small piece of land or support a few farm animals.

Murcia may seem to be something of a backwater at the moment but historically it differs in very few respects from anywhere else in Spain. The region was certainly inhabited during the Stone and Bronze Ages and has prehistoric caves and burial mounds. The Iberians, the Greeks, the Romans and the Moors built settlements there and several hamlets still have their original names, dating from the time when they were part of Al-Andalus. Following its recapture by Jaume I in the thirteenth century, Murcia became a Castilian outpost where Christians, Moors and Jews lived in comparative harmony while Aragon siezed one or two areas round the edge, thereby cutting the province down to its present size. During the sixteenth and seventeenth centuries Murcia was hit by floods, earthquakes and the plague but its agriculture continued to flourish and exports of silk, wool, minerals and fruit helped to keep its head above water. The area suffered very little during the War of Succession but was bedevilled by internal problems and political instability up to and including the Civil War. Today the province is making the most of its assets; improving its roads, protecting its wildlife and developing a pleasant holiday image.

Just across the border from Alicante, on the main coastal highway, the first town reached is **San Pedro del Pinatar**. This one-time harbour has some ancient salt mines in the vicinity and thermal baths originally used by the Moorish kings which are now a focal point for people suffering from rheumatism. There are a couple of modest .hotels, a furnished apartment or two, a hermitage which has been turned into the parish church and a Maritime Museum that can be visited by simply telephoning for an appointment (see the Additional Information section at the end of the chapter).

San Javier, a few kilometres down the road, is a bit livelier due, no doubt, to the presence of the Spanish Air Force Academy. The roadside verges outside the town are liberally planted with signs inviting motorists to play mini-golf or bingo, go to a disco, book in at a motel or visit the beaches at Santiago de la Ribera with its Real Club de Regatas and a small marina. The airport nearby is in daily contact with Madrid and has facilities for charter flights. There is a well equipped campsite overlooking the water with a bar, cafeteria, a shop, beach umbrellas and opportunities for fishing and subaqua. Another site in the vicinity has bungalows to rent, a swimming pool and facilities for tennis and riding as well as for doing the laundry or washing the car.

Los Alcázares, a small spa with a long history, is thought to have been the site of a Greek settlement before the Arabs moved in and

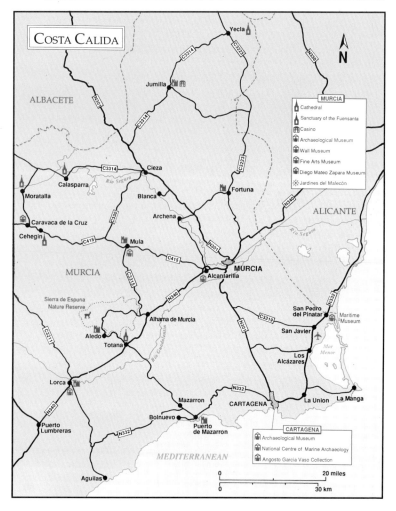

started building their own mansions. They called the community 'The Stately Homes' — *Al-Kazár* being the name for either a palace or a palatial residence. This hardly applies nowadays because Los Alcázares is an unassuming little place, looking out over the vast,

Opposite: The Club Náutico in La Manga is a popular night spot (top);
The modern market in La Unión is built to a traditional style (bottom)

salty expanse of the Mar Menor, with a background of lemon and almond trees, palms and an occasional windmill that twirls its collection of small, individual sails over one shoulder, rather like a tattered parasol. The town's main interest is in agriculture and its most important festival, the Semana de la Huerta, or 'Country Week', is held there every August.

South of Los Alcázares a minor road branches off from the main highway to follow the shoreline of the lagoon through little waterside resorts like Los Urrutias and Los Nietos, eventually joining forces with the MU312 for the final approach to the holiday playground of **La Manga**. It is thought that the Mar Menor was originally a small bay tucked in behind the rocky Cabo de Palos but that a sandbank gradually built up across the entrance, isolating it completely. This was christened La Manga, or 'The Sleeve', sluices and canals were cut to provide outlets to the sea and plans were laid to turn the massive spit into a tourist resort. The idea succeeded admirably as first class hotels and highrise apartment blocks appeared in rapid succession, with small houses built on piles, swimming pools, shops, discos, night spots, open-air cafés and restaurants. The Club Náutico was founded and a casino was opened. Water sports of all descriptions are available, either along the sandy beaches fringing the Mediterranean or a stone's throw away on the edge of the lagoon where the water is warmer and the waves are merely ripples. Golfing enthusiasts are just as well catered for at the La Manga Golf Course near Los Belones on the far side of the bridge that marks the entrance to the resort. It not only has thirty-six holes, tennis courts and a swimming pool, but also a hotel, furnished apartments, a bar and a restaurant.

Back on the main highway, beyond Los Belones, **La Union** is the comparatively modern centre of an ancient mining area with no hotels of any particular merit but two attractive Modernist buildings, namely the Casa del Piñón and the market where the Cante de las Minas, the Festival of Mining Songs, is held during the first week in August. The ore is shipped out through Portman, 9km (5$^1/_2$ miles) away along a narrow, twisting road through arid country where red earth, yellow sulphur deposits and the grey tones of its lead content blend together to create an arresting landscape. The whole coastline is rocky with a series of little bays and inlets, most of which are deserted because they are so difficult to reach. However, another minor road presses on to Escombreras with its modern oil refinery and from there continues to Cartagena. The city can be reached in a fraction of the time along the main road from La Union.

Cartagena, ideally situated on its own attractive bay and protected by a series of promontories, took its name from the Carthaginians who captured the existing settlement in 223BC. The port was developed by the Romans but largely ignored by the Moors in favour of Almería. The Christians only built a series of small forts on the surrounding hills. Later it was turned into a naval dockyard, provided with an important arsenal and played its part in the various upheavals which led to the Civil War. It has recently expanded quite considerably and now concentrates on commerce and industry while still preserving a few reminders of the past. The old quarter, with its narrow streets and somewhat dilapidated houses, is behind the Alfonso XIII dock, along the Calle Mayor and the Calle de los Cuatro Santos which used to be the port's main thoroughfares. The area is dominated by the former Castillo de la Concepción, now surrounded by public gardens and near the Romanesque cathedral that was virtually destroyed during the Civil War. It overlooks the port, the enormous Arsenal and the esplanade where an historic little submarine is surrounded by trees, flowers and souvenir stalls. It was designed by a local naval officer, Lieutenant Isaac Peral, and launched in 1888, powered by two electric engines of 30hp each. Other ancient fortresses with a commanding view of the harbour include the ruined Castillo de los Moros, the Castillo de la Atalaya, in a marginally better state of repair, and the Castillo de San Juan. The Castillo de Galeras with its encircling ramparts, Classical entrance and pepperpot lookout towers, was restored and turned into a military prison and is not open to the public.

Cartagena could never be accused of flaunting its tourist attractions, several of which are quite hard to find. Part of a Roman causeway has been left underneath a savings bank where it is incorporated into the small La Caja de Ahorros de Alicante y Murcia Collection on the Calle Conde Duque. Vestiges of Roman pavements appear in the most unlikely places such as the Plaza de los Tres Reyes, La Linterna is an ancient Moorish tower and a section of the walls built by Philip II still cling tenaciously to the hillside. There are Baroque altarpieces in churches like La Iglesia de Santo Domingo where a traditional crucifix is replaced by a large, robed figure of Christ carrying His cross. The dark thirteenth-century Virgen del Rosell is enthroned in the church of Santa María de Gracia while the Iglesia de la Caridad and its Capille de las Animas are filled with colourful statues by artists of the calibre of Francisco Salzillo. Modernist buildings include the town hall, the Aguirre Palace and the Casa Maestre, with their ornamental façades and the Casa

Above: Cartagena Town Hall; Below: The world's first electrically powered submarine, Cartagena

Llagostera, decorated with large ceramic murals of Mercury and Minerva, who bears a striking resemblance to Britannia.

The Archaeological Museum in the Calle Ramón y Cajal, established in 1982, is full of items from the early days of Cartagena, ranging from an exquisite Grecian golden earring to mosaics, artefacts, stone work and statues discovered in the vicinity. The National Centre of Marine Archaeological Investigations is both a museum and a research centre on the Dique de Navidad, in the port area. The exhibits include a Roman galley in an excellent state of preservation. There are models, pictures, archives and other documents as well as items going back to the days of the Phoenicians. These are augmented by fresh discoveries made by the resident team of scubadivers. The Angosto Garcia Vaso Collection concentrates on glassware and ceramics produced in the local mills and factories during the nineteenth century. It is privately owned and can only be visited by appointment (see the Additional Information).

One of the city's most illustrious citizens is Pedro Marina Cartagena. He receives a salary of 55,000 pesetas a month from the naval dockyard but does no work whatsoever and, on the rare occasions when he ventures out onto the streets, he is always surrounded by large crowds. The simple explanation is that Pedro is the figure of St Peter who plays a major part in the Holy Week celebrations, said to be among the most memorable in Spain.

Cartagena has one comfortable hotel and several smaller but quite adequate establishments as well as furnished apartments and a first class campsite which has facilities for tennis, mini-golf, fishing and diving as well as a swimming pool, a restaurant, a shop and a laundrette. Despite this, and the fact that there are plenty of restaurants in the city, many holidaymakers choose to stay in Puerto de Mazarrón, some 40km (25 miles) further down the coast.

Puerto de Mazarrón has the same variety of hotels and furnished apartments as Cartagena, as well as private villas and pleasant sandy beaches, interrupted by rocky outcrops. The nearby attractions include a ruined castle and the church of San Andrés in its parent village about 7km (4 miles) from the coast and a collection of weird rock formations known as the Enchanted City of Bolnuevo, about 5km (3 miles) away along a minor road that runs beside the bay.

A secondary road, linked to the foreshore by country lanes, connects Mazarrón with **Aguilas**, the last port on the Costa Cálida. It was known as *Urci* during the Arab occupation but was renamed San Juan de Aguilas after the reconquest and then more or less abandoned in the face of repeated attacks by pirates from North

Africa. In 1765 the Count of Aranda, acting on orders from Carlos III, set about restoring the castle, repairing the fortifications and improving the port facilities. Today it concerns itself with fishing, growing tomatoes, establishing campsites and developing its tourist image. From Aguilas a coast road heads south across the border into Almería while the only other secondary route sets off for the interior, linking the port with both Puerto Lumbreras and Lorca. The surrounding hills form a landscape that would be extremely arid without the man-made terraces planted with tomatoes and covered in enormous plastic sheets. Nearly every little wayside café and isolated homestead has its own minute garden, bright with roses and hibiscus, shaded by orange trees and surrounded by cacti and prickly pears. **Puerto Lumbreras** is an excellent place to stop on the way south to Andalucía with the result that its modern, well-appointed *parador* can be very crowded, especially at the height of the season. However, there are other hotels and *hostales* in the town as well as restaurants and a campsite that is convenient for travellers staying overnight but has little to recommend it for longer periods.

Puerto Lumbreras has nothing in the way of tourist attractions, apart from a collection of troglodyte dwellings carved out of the hillside near the road to Granada, but **Lorca**, 18km (11 miles) away on the main route to Murcia, has been declared a national monument. It is an attractive market town in the unexpectedly fertile valley of the Río Guadalentín, dominated by the remains of an Arab fortress that played an important supporting role during the reconquest of Granada. Much of this has crumbled away but two towers, the Alfonsina and the Espolón, have been restored and can be reached, without too much effort, from the Plaza de España. The square itself is overlooked by the town hall, an elderly palace which is now the law courts, and the collegiate church of San Patricio which started life in 1554 and has its full quota of religious statues. The surrounding area is a delightful maze of little streets, most of which are closed to traffic and lined with old houses that peer out on passers by through heavy wrought iron grilles. The Casa de los Guervara on the Calle Lope Gisbert is a one-time palace with a Baroque doorway and a charming, decorative patio. It is the home of both the Tourist Office and the Lorca Museum whose contents range from archaeological exhibits to embroidery, ethnology and sacred art. The town is famous for its spectacular Holy Week festivities. Richly costumed Romans on beautiful horses, biblical characters, pilgrims and members of the White and Blue Brotherhoods have their traditional places in the procession of floats, each trying to outdo the others in a spirit of rivalry that has existed for centuries. The town boasts a number of other old churches and mansions, a wide range of hotels and plenty of cafés and restaurants but the nearest campsite is at Totana further up the road.

Although **Totana** is an ancient town, it could hardly be described as a tourist resort because there are so few hotels. However, there are more cafés and restaurants than one would expect, an unusual fountain, a sixteenth-century parish church with a fine Mudejar ceiling and the sanctuary of Santa Eulalia on the slopes of the Sierra de Espuña, 7km (4 miles) to the north-west. This is an area of wild, open country, the haunt of golden eagles and great bearded vultures. From the nearby village of **Aledo**, a medieval stronghold with the partly restored remnants of a hilltop fortress and a church full of statues and sculptures, a scenic road makes a couple of wide sweeps through the nature reserve. The shorter of the two can spring some unwelcome surprises on the way to **Alhama de Murcia** so less adventurous motorists would undoubtedly prefer to cover the 12km (7 miles) from Totana along the main route. Once there, the attractions are somewhat muted, consisting of a few traces of a Bronze Age settlement, thermal springs that were frequented by the Romans, the stark ruins of an Arab castle and the church of San Lazaro.

Alcantarilla, on the outskirts of the provincial capital, is known chiefly for its enormous wheel, designed by the Moors, that scoops up water from the main canal and deposits it in an irrigation channel running along the top. It is part of the Huerta Museum where a number of typical thatched farmhouses have been reconstructed among the orange and lemon groves, palm trees and gardens. A relatively modern building is filled to capacity with appropriate furniture, pottery, glasswork, implements and utensils, hand-looms, traditional costumes and accessories, musical instruments and even bed clothes. There is also a library and a restaurant surrounded by trees within easy reach of the main entrance.

Alcantarilla was an Iberian settlement before it passed into the hands of the Muslim queen Al-Hora and subsequently those of the queens of Castile before being destroyed by a flood in 1545. A replacement town was built on a site close by, which accounts for the fact that it is now more industrial than historic with nothing apart from the museum in the way of tourist attractions. However, anyone with a few hours to spare might well enjoy a trip up into the mountains to visit Mula, Cehegin and Caravaca de la Cruz.

It is less than 30km (20 miles) along the C415 to **Mula** which is surrounded by farmlands and gives its name to the local river. An imposing castle rises up out of some spectacular rocks on the hilltop and is worth a visit if only for the view. Apart from some old buildings and the nearby Cierva reservoir, there is a small museum which exhibits discoveries made by archaeologists at the Iberian shrine and necropolis of Cigarralejo. **Cehegín** also has a ruined castle poised above the Río Argos, an ancient quarter with narrow streets that have hardly changed since the days of the Visigoths, and the sixteenth-century church of La Magdalena. It is a sombre building, much restored about 100 years ago, which keeps its treasures in a Museum of Religious Art in the vestry. They include some gold and silver articles and a Renaissance carving of Santa Maria Magdalena, whose robes lost nearly all their colour when she stood outside in a niche over the heavy wooden door. The Archaeological Museum in the old town hall delves back into prehistory and there are exhibits from the Peña Rubia caves and several reminders of the Visigoths.

The museums in **Caravaca de la Cruz** cover a wide range of subjects. The site has been inhabited since the Bronze Age, the Iberians and the Romans settled there and it belonged to the Knights Templar and later to the Order of Santiago. However, its most enduring legend dates back to the Moorish occupation when the king apparently asked a priest called Ginés Pérez Chirinos to celebrate mass because he wanted to see what was involved. Everything had been prepared when Chirinos realised that the cross was missing; at that moment it reappeared on the altar, the king was converted to Christianity and the word spread that angels had provided one made from part of the True Cross. Unfortunately, this is said to have been stolen during the Civil War and when no second heavenly replacement was forthcoming, the Vatican sent a substitute containing a sliver from the Lignum Crucis. The vestments Chirinos is reputed to have worn on that occasion in 1231 are preserved in a glass case in the Museum of Religious Art and History. The museum is housed in the ornate seventeenth-century Real Alcázar-Santuario de la Santisima y Vera Cruz in the grounds of the castle. One room is devoted to paintings while the other, known as the Old Vestry, is hung with tapestries and contains a large number of precious items such as a Baroque chalice, a finely-worked monstrance-reliquary and an eighteenth-century coffer.

The Ethnological Museum on the Calle Gobernador Izarra is much more down to earth; full of equipment used by various craftsmen and farm workers such as threshing machines, spinning wheels and contraptions for beating hemp as well as harnesses and pieces of local pottery. The Soledad Museum, tucked away in an ancient church on the Calle Eugenio D'ors, concerns itself with articles from the distant past, augmented by maps and photographs showing exactly where each one was discovered. Last, but by no means least, the closed convent of San José, an Order founded by Santa Teresa in 1576, has its own Museum of Sacred Art. It includes exhibits ranging from statues of San José and the Virgin Mary (which were presents from Santa Teresa) to documents signed by St John of the Cross who paid several visits to the town and addressed the nuns at the convent. Caravaca de la Cruz insists that an unusually high percentage of its houses date from around the Middle Ages but there are very few interesting buildings clustered below the walls of its magnificently preserved castle. It is possible to find a modest *hostal* and a few small restaurants but nothing in the way of other tourist accommodation or even a campsite in the surrounding area.

For dedicated sightseers, every village in the area has its own particular attractions, either scenic or man-made. **Moratalla**, 14km (9 miles) to the north has a number of ruins, a church, a convent and a variety of wildlife on the doorstep. **Calasparra** has rice paddies surrounding the sanctuary of Nuestra Señora de la Esperanza, which is hewn out of solid rock and is a well known place of pilgrimage. It is only a short distance from the source of the Río Segura, an attractive rivulet swollen by both the Argos and the Quipar on its way to Cieza. This is an historic little town conveniently sited on the main road from Albacete to Murcia. Here the main attractions include prehistoric caves, castle ruins and two churches.

The N301 follows the course of the Segura, bypassing Blanca, known principally for its citrus orchards and bull-running through the streets as in Pamplona. It also bypasses Archena where the thermal baths are surrounded by gardens and freshwater terraces. The road and the river come together at Molina de Segura and then go their separate ways to **Murcia**.

Although this city is not one of the most outstanding provincial capitals in Spain, it is pleasant and friendly, with clean, wide streets, fairly modern buildings, plenty of trees and its full quota of tourist attractions. There are more than enough hotels in every category from first class, to modest pensions, dozens of different shops and restaurants but very little furnished accommodation. The nearest airport is at San Javier on the Mar Menor and there are train services to Madrid, Barcelona, Valencia and Albacete as well as some of the larger provincial towns, augmented by coaches to places as far afield as Granada, Sevilla and Málaga. Local buses keep in touch with the villages and coastal resorts in addition to a daily service to La Manga.

Murcia started life as *Mursiya* in AD831, after the surrounding marshlands had been drained and the reigning Arab potentate decided that it would be ideal as the centre of a small Moorish kingdom. It was recovered by the Christians in 1266, after which the city kept a low profile, concentrating on agriculture and the manufacture of silk until quite recently when commerce and industry were added to its other accomplishments. The old quarter, with its atmospheric medieval streets and historic buildings, lies on either side of the river and extends roughly from the bullring to the dual carriageway on the road from Albacete to Cartagena.

The cathedral, more or less in the centre of the old town, has a splendidly ornate Baroque façade overlooking the fountain in the Plaza del Cardenal Belluga and a magnificent view from the belfry for anyone willing to negotiate a series of ramps and climb the slightly claustrophobic spiral stairway to the top. Two other entrances worth inspecting are the fifteenth-century Puerta de los Apóstoles and the Puerta de las Cadenas facing the Calle de la Trapería which was the main thoroughfare in medieval times. The interior of the cathedral is mainly Gothic, dating from the early fifteenth century when it replaced a mosque which had been converted to Christianity after the reconquest. It took a considerable time to build, which means there are many variations in both style and treatment. The Capilla de los Vélez is especially memorable, profusely decorated behind a tracery of carved stone work and heavy wrought iron gates, while the Capilla de Junterón presents a more Classical face but is equally elaborate. The carved sixteenth-century choir stalls came from an ancient Castilian monastery and there is some beautiful panelling on the far side of the Plateresque doors leading to the sacristy. The chapter house and part of the cloister are filled with treasures, the oldest being the intricately carved Sarcophagus of the Muses dating from the third century AD. As well as Gothic statues and interesting altarpieces, there is a magnificent figure of San Jerónimo by Francisco Salzillo, generally considered to be his masterpiece. There are also an enormous silver monstrance and an impressive array of religious artifacts as well as documents signed by people like Sancho IV and Alfonso the Wise whose innards are said to be preserved in an urn on the main altar.

About a block and a half away, down the Calle de la Tapería, the Casino is a private club which holds periodical exhibitions and also welcomes casual sightseers. Built at the turn of the century, it is one of the most sumptuous in Spain with a ballroom inspired by the Palace of Versailles, decorative archways that would not look out of place in the Alhambra and a long hall with comfortable furniture and an eye-catching glass roof. At the far end of the street is the Plaza de Santo Domingo and beyond it the city's Archaeological Museum. This pleasant, rather conventional building is full of interesting items beginning with urns and funeral accessories discovered in the region's prehistoric burial grounds. The Iberians are represented by votive offerings and odd little figures like the so-called Lady of Cehegin, while the Romans have contributed everything from statues and mosaics to ceramics and a copy of the altar from Monte Sacro de Cartagena which was transferred to Barcelona some time ago. The Moors have their own section, spanning nearly seven centuries. Here, the fine collection of ceramics includes an unusual bird bath designed along the lines of a twin-towered Arab fortress.

The Fine Arts Museum is quite a walk away on the Calle Obispo Frutos, a block or two from the bullring. The drawings and paintings are interesting but little compares with the Salzillo Museum in the church of Jesus on the Calle San Andrés at the opposite end of the old town. The exceptional tableaux he created for the Brotherhood of Jesus, which are carried in procession through the city on Good Friday morning, can be seen in the side chapels. The most memorable of these are the Last Supper, with the bearded apostles grouped casually round the table set with fruit and candles, the Betrayal in the Garden of Gethsemane, and St John and the Angel. There is also a beautiful Nativity tableau as well as dozens of little figurines; some are biblical, others depict mid-eighteenth century peasant life .

Other local collections include the International Museum of Traditional Folk Costumes, the Wall Museum on the site of an ancient fortified gateway containing maps of Murcia as it was before the reconquest, and items of eighteenth-century sacred art in the Diego Mateo Zapara Museum. These are displayed in the body of the parish church near the choir stalls and include sculptures, paintings and silverware as well as richly embroidered canopies and altar cloths. Many other small churches and a few monasteries are also open to visitors, sometimes by appointment only, and range from the stark but impressive church of Santiago to the Iglesia Conventual de Santa Ana where the high altar practically drips with gold. Additional attractions include the university, the nineteenth-century Teatro de Romea, the large covered market and the Jardines del Malecón with its trees, lawns, fountains and modern sculptures known collectively as the Museo de Escultura al Aire Libre.

After its solemn Holy Week processions, Murcia goes to town with a Spring Festival that incorporates fancy dress parades, a battle of

Opposite: Murcia — the ornate Capilla de los Vélez in the cathedral (top), and Town Hall (bottom)

flowers, floats of all descriptions and even a ritual Sardine Funeral marking the end of Lent. Other provincial centres have their own highly individual ways of celebrating both religious and historic events. Lorca makes a feature of Cleopatra and her attendant slaves in the annual Triumph of Christianity fiesta while Caravaca highlights a horse race called the Caballos del Vino during the Santísima y Vera Cruz festivities in May. This recalls an ancient siege when the Knights Templar broke out through the Arab lines in search of water but failed to reach the wells and returned instead with wine skins snatched from the enemy.

Some 5km (3 miles) to the south-east of the capital, the sanctuary of the Fuensanta is the scene of a colourful annual pilgrimage which takes place during the first 2 weeks of September. The church was built more than 200 years ago near a cave where a beautiful actress called La Cómica suddenly gave up her career to become a penitent. The Virgin of the Sacred Fountain later replaced La Arrixaca as the patron saint of Murcia. The sixteenth-century figure made her permanent home in the sanctuary, dressed in richly embroidered robes and expensive jewellery, in keeping with her new surroundings. A scenic little road makes a detour round the sanctuary to the Cresta del Gallo, a jagged mountain crest. It is worth visiting for a series of panoramic views over Murcia and the bare hills thrown up by ancient volcanoes in the Sierra de Columbares.

The C3223, which takes leave of the main highway from Murcia to Orihuela at Los Pavos, skirts round the Embalse de Santomera to pay its respects to **Fortuna**, 25km (15 miles) from the capital. It is a popular little spa whose medicinal waters fill the swimming pools of the three local hotels, all of which have tennis courts and gardens as well. There are a few furnished apartments, about half a dozen typical restaurants and a campsite with a small shop and a cafeteria but no recreational facilities on the premises. However, the village has its obligatory castle ruins as well as a Baroque altarpiece and the Monstrance de las Espigas in the parish church.

From Fortuna a choice of minor roads wind their way through arid, sparsely populated country to the wine town of **Jumilla** which is encased in vineyards. The area all round is peppered with the remains of prehistoric settlements, vying for attention with the small Paleo-Christian burial ground of El Casón. This is near the convent of Santa Ana, isolated at the end of a small country lane with a few pine trees for company. The remains of an ancient castle spread themselves along the hilltop above the town. The encircling walls are punctuated by a series of small towers with a partly restored keep near the Puerta de los Musulmanes on the north side dominating the Patio de Armas and the adjacent hermitage of Santa María de Gracia.

Jumilla has very little to offer in the way of accommodation, few restaurants and no campsites. However, the town hall, known as La Cárcel (The Prison), is a Renaissance structure with a fetching gallery, while the church of Santiago has been declared a national monument. The Jerónimo Molina Archaeological Museum in the Plaza de la Constitución has carefully pieced together several examples of ancient pottery while an interesting contrast is provided by a second room full of archaeological forgeries, many of them the work of two famous gipsies, El Corro and El Rosao. A further section is devoted to tools and other equipment used in the past by farmers, craftsmen and tradespeople such as butchers and confectioners and yet another area to sacred art. The local Bodegas Carcelén has gathered together a Collection of Wine-cellar Equipment. This is a comprehensive selection of articles used for making wine with presses dating back to the fourteenth century, jars and measures and all the implements necessary for constructing the barrels.

Yecla, 28km (17 miles) to the north-east along the C3314, was once part of the kingdom of Castile. During the War of Succession it threw in its lot with Philip V and was attacked by Austrian troops who destroyed all the archives. The whitewashed houses, with their tiled roofs, are generally uniform and not very picturesque but there are a handful of small churches including the seventeenth-century Basilica de la Purisima and the church of San Francisco with a Dolorosa fashioned by Salzillo. The Archaeological Museum is less absorbing than the Museum of El Greco Reproductions by Juan Albert Roses, a local artist who completed the seventy-five canvases in 1953. They are amazingly true to the originals and have been on exhibition in cities as far apart as Athens and Havana.

Yecla is the last place of interest in Murcia, although geographically it is closer to the Costa Blanca than it is to the Costa Cálida. It is connected by a series of secondary roads to either Alicante or Benidorm while motorists on their way to the north can continue along the C3223 to Almansa where the N430 provides a direct link with Valencia and the Costa del Azahar.

Additional Information

Places of Interest

Alcantarilla
Huerta Museum
Carretera de Andalucia
Open: 10.30am-2pm and 4-9pm in
summer. 10.30-2pm and 4-8pm in
winter. ☎ 968 80 03 40

Caravaca de la Cruz
Ethnological Museum
Instituto Nacional de Bachillerato
Calle Gobernador Izarra
Open: during school hours. Closed
Sunday, public holidays and school
holidays. ☎ 70 06 04 or 70 07 32

Museum of Sacred Art
Monasterio de San José de Monjas
Carmelitas Delcalzas
Calle Mayor
Open: 10am-1pm and 4-6pm.
☎ 70 01 65

Museum of Religious Art and History
Real Alcázar-Santuario de la
Santisima y Vera Cruz
Open: 10am-1pm and 4-7pm.
☎ 70 07 43

Soledad Museum
Iglesia de la Soledad
Calle Eugenio D'ors
Open: 10am-2pm and 6-8pm.

Cartagena
Angosto Garcia Vaso Collection
Palma 1
Open: weekdays 4-6pm by
appointment only.
☎ 52 57 29

Archaeological Museum
Calle Ramón y Cajal
Open: 10am-1pm and 4-6pm.
Weekends 10am-1pm. Closed
Monday and holiday afternoons.

*La Caja de Ahorros de Alicante y
Murcia Collection*
Calle Conde Duque
Open during banking hours.
☎ 50 22 40

*National Centre of Marine Archaeo-
logical Investigations*
Dique de Navidad
Open: 10am-2pm and 5-7pm.
Closed Monday and public holiday
afternoons. ☎ 50 84 15

Cehegin
Archaeological Museum
The old town hall
Plaza de la Iglesia
Enquire at the town hall.

Museum of Religious Art
Iglesia de Santa María Magdalena
Open: during services, otherwise
by appointment. ☎ 74 00 40

Jumilla
Collection of Wine-cellar Equipment
Bodegas Carcelén
Open: during business hours.
☎ 78 04 18

*Jerónimo Molina Archaeological
Museum*
Plaza de la Constitución 3
Open: 11am-1pm and 5-7pm. Visit
by telephone appointment only.
☎ 78 00 36

Murcia
Casino
Visit on request
Enquire from the porter.

Cathedral Museum
In the cathedral
Salzillo 2
Open: 10am-12noon and 5-7.30pm.
☎ 21 63 44

Diego Mateo Zapara Museum
Parroquia de San Nicolás 1
Open: during services. Visit by
appointment only. ☎ 21 92 30

*International Museum of Traditional
Folk Costumes*
For full details enquire at the
Tourist Office (see below).

Archaeological Museum
Alfonso X el Sabio 7
Open: 9am-2pm July and August.
Closed Sunday and public
holidays. 10am-2pm and 6-8pm in
winter. 11am-2pm Saturday and
Sunday. Closed Monday.
☎ 23 46 02

Fine Arts Museum
Obispo Frutos 12
Open: 9am-2pm July and August.
Closed Sunday and holidays.
Otherwise 10am-2pm and 5-7pm
Tuesday to Friday. 11am-2pm
Saturday and Sunday. Closed
Monday. ☎ 23 93 46

Salzillo Museum
San Andrés 1
Open: 9.30am-1pm and 4-7pm in
summer. 9.30am-1pm and 3-6pm in
winter. 10am-1pm on holidays.

Wall Museum
Plaza de Santa Eulalia
For visiting hours enquire at the
Tourist Office (see below).

San Pedro del Pinatar
Maritime Museum
Cofradía de Pescadores
Visit by appointment. ☎ 57 19 20

Yecla
Archaeological Museum
Plaza de los Ortega
Open: 9.30am-12.30pm and 5-9pm
on weekdays. Closed Saturday and
Sunday. ☎ 79 00 46

Museum of El Greco Reproductions
Plaza de los Ortega
Open: 9.30am-12.30pm and 5-9pm
weekdays. Closed Saturday and
Sunday.
☎ 79 00 46

Tourist Offices

Aguilas
Av. José Antonio 20
☎ 41 29 63

Cartagena
Ayuntamiento
☎ 50 64 83
Calle de Castellini 5
☎ 50 75 49

La Manga
Plaza Bohemia
☎ 56 30 96 or 56 37 24

Los Alcazares
Carretera de San Javier
☎ 57 52 79 (also for Mar Menor)

Murcia
Calle de Alejandro Séiquer 4
☎ 21 37 16
Calle Tomás Maestre
☎ 21 61 15
Calle Junterones 14
☎ 24 26 77

Puerto de Mazarron
Calle San Hilario
☎ 59 45 08 or 50 44 34

Santiago de la Ribera
Paseo de Colón
☎ 57 11 16

San Pedro del Pinatar
Avinguda Dr Artero Guirao
☎ 18 23 01

Spain: Fact File

Accommodation

Of all the different types of accommodation available in Spain, the best-known are undoubtedly the *paradores*, a nationwide system of comfortable, well-equipped hotels run by the State and situated less than 1 day's drive apart. Visitors can tour the entire country, staying for the most part in historic palaces, castles and convents. To avoid leaving any awkward gaps in the chain they have been augmented with new hotels in areas where the existing accommodation was either very limited or not entirely suitable. There are some eighty *paradores* in all, the most elaborate being the most expensive, but all of them are guaranteed to provide first class amenities, excellent service and interesting traditional menus. The eastern costas have eight *paradores* between them — at Aiguablava, Vic, Cardona, Tortosa, Benicarlo, El Saler, Javea, and Puerto Lumbreras. There are also three more in the Catalan Pyrénées.

Apart from the *paradores*, the hotels range from luxurious five-star establishments down to the basic one-star variety which may well not have any private bathrooms or public lounges and almost certainly no lift. The *hostales* are also star-rated but usually correspond to hotels in the grade below, while the term *residencia* indicates that there is no dining room although they may provide breakfast and occasionally have a cafeteria. All the hotels and *hostales* are government controlled and have blue plaques at the main entrance giving their official status. A list of prices must be displayed in the lobby so it is possible to see at a glance if a room has a bath or only a shower. It is a good idea to look before you book in case there is some hidden drawback, such as windows opening onto a busy road. All except one-star *hostales* have heating installed and frequently provide extra blankets.

In the unlikely event of any serious difficulties, guests can always ask for the complaints book, or *libro de reclamaciones* and all entries must be shown to the authorities immediately. This means trouble for the proprietor so the management will usually prefer to put things right and so avoid an official black mark. Unless otherwise stated, the prices are for two people sharing a double room. Anyone on their own will pay more than 50 per cent of the price but if a third bed is available it will only cost about one third more. Many hotels make reductions for young children but as this is at the discretion of the management it is necessary to agree the terms in advance. Breakfast is nearly always extra and 6 per cent VAT is added to the overall bill. Guests who have to watch the pesetas should remember this and pay for drinks rather than ask for them to be charged to the number of the room.

Some of the larger towns and established holiday resorts provide furnished accommodation, which may be either a villa or an apartment, while quite a few campsites also have bungalows to rent. The sites themselves are graded according to the amenities, from luxury, followed by classes 1, 2 and 3, the most downmarket of which have nothing very much to offer but are quite adequate for an overnight stop. There are dozens in all shapes and sizes massed along the coast although they tend to thin out quite considerably south of Alicante as well as becoming rather few and far between the further you travel inland. There are also a few youth hostels (*albergues juveniles*) but they are not always conveniently sited and may close during the winter. It is generally more agreeable, and sometimes less expensive, to find a room in a small hotel or pension. Long distance hikers can also camp out in one of the mountain refuges, which cost nothing, but in this case it is necessary to arrive fully equipped with everything you need, including sleeping bags.

Climate

The climate along the eastern costas of Spain varies quite considerably. The coastal resorts of the Costa Brava are usually very pleasant with fairly mild winters and agreeably warm summers that seldom become too hot or humid. However, the foothills of the Pyrénées extend over a large part of the interior and as the highest peaks are covered in snow for up to 6 months of the year the inland centres tend to vary from cool to cold with the temperatures in some ski resorts dropping as low as -20°C.

The Costa del Maresme follows much the same pattern as the Costa Brava along the coast but is far enough south to avoid most of the inland snow, which means that the winter temperatures seldom drop to more than a few degrees below zero. Barcelona admits officially to 33°C in the high summer and -7°C in the depths of winter. Temperatures at the northern end of the Costa Daurada correspond to those of the

Weather Information

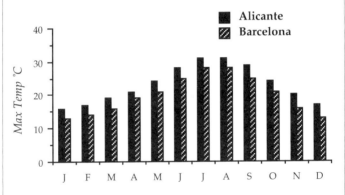

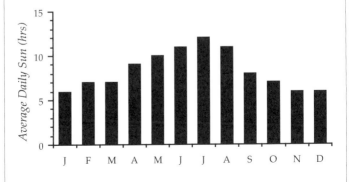

Costa del Maresme but they have a tendency to even out towards the Delta de l'Ebre where the average fluctuation is between 10 °C in January and 27 °C during August. The late spring and late autumn are often wet but otherwise the area is extremely dry and there are high winds during the winter. The Costa del Azahar is slightly warmer but can be subject to widespread flooding any time from November to April. In summer it may be rather sultry.

The Costa Blanca claims to have the best all-the-year-round weather of any coast in Spain, including the Costa del Sol. The summers are hot and the winters warm but the brochures fail to mention the slight possibility of earth tremors, mainly in the triangle formed by Santa Pola, Torrevieja and Orihuela. Finally the Costa Cálida is well named, it is warm in winter when the water temperature in the Mar Menor hovers around 18 °C, and can be sweltering in summer, particularly in the semi-desert area that borders on Andalucía.

Credit Cards

Most large hotels and restaurants, especially in the main towns and popular tourist resorts, accept one or more of the major credit cards. The relevant logo is usually displayed in the window or at the reception desk but it is worth confirming in advance. Some garages, particularly in large towns and along the main highways, also take credit cards but very few others will accept them, nor will the majority of supermarkets. Some banks will pay out against a credit card, most will accept a Eurocheque and change travellers cheques.

Currency

Any amount of foreign currency may be taken into Spain but only limited quantities of either pesetas or other currencies may be taken out again, unless it can be proved that any excess was brought in initially. As the specific amounts may change it is always wise to obtain expert advice if several hundred pounds or dollars are involved. The exchange rate fluctuates so it is impossible to give an exact figure but a useful yardstick is to look on the green 1,000 peseta note as the equivalent of about £5 or $7.50.

Customs Regulations

The customs regulations in Spain are similar to those in force elsewhere in the EEC. If you are in any doubt it is as well to check before leaving.

Dress

The rules governing dress in Spain have been relaxed considerably with the growth of tourism. Topless bathing is quite acceptable and there are several nudist areas. Care should be taken not to give offence when visiting churches, convents and monasteries although visitors are no longer expected to cover their heads or wear stockings. Low heeled shoes are essential for anyone who is planning to explore cobbled streets, while rubber boots and muted colours are necessary in the marshy reserves. A warm jersey and a light raincoat can both come in very useful.

Electricity

The usual voltage is 220 or 225 AC although there are some places that still operate on 110 or 125 volts. Adaptors will be needed by anyone who does not use European continental two-pin plugs at home.

Health Care

Visitors covered by British National Insurance can expect to benefit under the Spanish Health Service as long as they have an E111 form with them. However, it is wise to have additional insurance, which is essential for nearly everybody else. All the usual services are available and pharmacies (these are called *farmacias* and can be identified by a green cross) can usually deal with minor problems or suggest the best place to go for assistance. Most well-known medicines are available in the large towns and tourist resorts but anything which needs a doctor's prescription at home will not be supplied without one.

Language

Both Castilian and local Spanish are spoken on the costas of Catalunya and Valencia and even in the resorts, where a percentage of the population have a working knowledge of English, any modest attempt — such as good morning (*buenos dias*), please (*por favor*) and thank you *(gracias)* — is both polite and appreciated. A phrase book and a dictionary are useful when venturing off the beaten track.

Metrication

1 kilo (1000g) = 2.2lb
1 litre = $1^3/_4$ pints
4.5 litres = 1 gallon
8 kilometres = 5 miles

Opening Hours

Many of the banks in Spain are open 6 days a week — usually from 9am-2pm on weekdays and 9am-12.30 or 1pm on Saturdays. However, the smaller, out-of-town branches may close earlier on Saturdays or perhaps not open at all. Post offices, like shops, tend to close for lunch, which lasts from about 1.30pm to 4.30pm or even 5pm, but stamps are available from the local tobacconist. Supermarkets generally stay open all day and the shops are usually open 9am-1pm Monday to Saturday and seldom close before 7.30 or 8pm.

Some churches are open during services, and others are prepared to admit visitors except during services. The remainder may observe office hours, list their opening and closing times, vary them without any warning, or not open at all in which case it is necessary to find the sacristan. He is seldom very far away and will usually produce the key in return for a modest contribution to the church funds, provided he is not disturbed at lunchtime or too late in the evening.

Apart from the main museums and places of interest in the larger towns and cities, it is almost impossible to predict future opening and closing times. However, as a general rule, most places close for a lengthy lunch at about 1.30pm and stay open a little longer on summer evenings than they do in winter. It is as well to check with the tourist office if a longish journey is involved but it is fairly safe to assume that nearly everywhere is closed on Monday.

Passports

A valid, up-to-date passport is the only document necessary for entry into Spain for citizens of more than fifty different countries including Britain, Canada and the United States. Extensions are granted for visitors who plan to stay for more than 3 months.

Public Holidays

Spain has about eleven or twelve public holidays a year. Most places also have two or more local holidays, possibly in honour of a patron saint or to commemorate some important occasion. Banks and public offices are closed on public holidays but certain shops, especially in the main tourist resorts, may stay open.

New Year's Day
6 January (Epiphany)
Maundy Thursday (The Thursday before Easter)
Good Friday
Easter Monday
1 May (Labour Day)
Corpus Christi
25 July (St James' Day)
15 August (Assumption)
11 September (National Day in Catalunya)
12 October (Spanish National Day)
1 November (All Saints Day)
6 December (Constitution Day)
8 December (Immaculate Conception)
25 December
26 December

Souvenirs

Along the costas of Catalunya the things to look for are pottery and glassware, wrought iron and wood, whereas Barcelona has clothes and leather goods, antiques, pictures and jewellery. On the Costa del Azahar ceramics, basketware, glass and toys are popular and not expensive. However, there are also beautiful hand-painted fans, guitars, silk, Morocco leather and even small pieces of furniture.

The Costa Blanca offers a variety of pottery, some of which is glazed although the plain white jugs are ideal for keeping water cool. Among other items available are blankets, wrought iron, articles decorated with sea shells and little ships sparkling with salt crystals. The most unusual souvenirs on the Costa Cálida are small figurines almost identical to the ones created by Salzillo and rare pieces of embroidery that can sometimes be bought in specialist artisan workshops. Baskets and blankets are easier to come by, along with pottery including jugs that are faithful reproductions of medieval designs.

Sports and Pastimes

Climbing and Speleology

Mountain climbing is a popular pastime in the foothills of the Pyrénées, especially in areas like Mount Pedraforce in Catalunya. Valencia has a special mountaineering excursion centre in the Calle Caballeros (☎ 331 16 43) and there are caves to explore in the north of Alicante province.

Cycling

The eastern costas can be quite pleasant for cycling if the weather is neither too hot nor too wet. There are some bicycles for hire whereas visitors who prefer to take their own can make arrangements to put them on the train, but transporting them by air is rather more complicated.

Fishing

Fishing is a popular sport all along the costas, both inland for salmon, trout and other freshwater varieties and from rocks or boats on the coast where underwater fishing conditions can be excellent, especially along the Costa del Azahar and

the Costa Blanca. Anyone planning to explore caves below
the waterline should remember to take an immersion lantern. There are rules and regulations governing such things
as the size of the catch and open and closed seasons, and in
some cases it is necessary to have a licence. All the relevant
details are available from the National Institute for the
Conservation of Nature (ICONA) which has provincial
headquarters in most of the large towns. Applications for
licences must include your name, address and passport
number as well as a cheque in pesetas, drawn on a local bank.
Valencia also has a Fishing Federation in the Calle Salvador
(☎ 331 86 10). There is also an informative brochure, available
from the Spanish Tourist Office, called *Fishing. Spain* which
is very useful.

Golf

Golfers will find several different courses at fairly regular
intervals all the way from the Costa Brava to the Mar Menor.
Some have nine holes, others eighteen, as well as one or two
with thirty-six; most have restaurants and perhaps small
shops, tennis courts and swimming pools in addition to
equipment for hire. Many, but not all, are open throughout
the year.

Hunting and Shooting

There are facilities for hunting and shooting in National
Reserves, private preserves and on common land for which
both licences and hunting insurance are obligatory.

Two companies on the eastern costas organise hunting
expeditions. One is in Barcelona province at the Centro de
Información Cinegética, Vingeu de Montserrat 38, Pineda de
Mar (☎ 207 15 88) and the other at Cacerias Orojeo, La
Caverada s/n, Estartit on the Costa Brava. Valencia's Hunting Federation is in the Plaza Cánovas del Castillo 8 (☎ 334 83
63). The term 'big game' refers to animals like deer, wild boar
and ibex while 'small game' includes rabbits, hares, water
fowl and different types of birds. Certain species are protected, among them lynx, some Spanish goats, bustards and
buzzards and eagles. As with fishing, all the necessary information, and a licence to hunt on common land, can be
obtained from ICONA who require a name, address and
passport number with the application and a cheque to cover

the fee. Each province has its own headquarters; Barcelona's is at Roberto Bassas 22 y 24 (☎ 321 13 29) and Valencia has one at San Vicente 83 (☎ 322 50 04).

The hunting seasons vary very little from year to year, certain types of guns are prohibited and a permit must be obtained by anyone intending to bring weapons of their own into the country. *Hunting. Spain* is a useful brochure and is obtainable from the Spanish Tourist Office.

Walking

Apart from many local areas, such as the various nature reserves which have their own marked footpaths for bird watchers and people who want to explore in the immediate vicinity, long distance walkers have several routes to choose from, both inland and along the coast. Refuges have been built beside some of the mountain trails and the best way to get detailed information is to write to the Spanish Mountaineering Federation at Alberto Aguilera 3-4, Madrid 15 (☎ 445 13 82).

It is very easy to set out from France or Andorra and follow the familiar international signs and symbols through the sierras of Catalunya into either Aragon or Valencia. Volunteers who belong to hiking clubs all over the country help to maintain the long distance footpaths, none of which present any real problems although it is essential to wear strong boots, carry a full waterbottle and have a detailed map and waterproof clothing. Walking maps may be obtained from Habilitado del Instituto, Geografico y Catastral, General Ibañez de Ibero 3, Madrid. Some local tourist offices will also supply them.

Ramblers in search of a little gentle exercise will find blazed nature footpaths in the Delta de l'Ebre and in the volcanic region round Olot, a lagoon trail in the Empordá marches, country walks up in the sierras and vast stretches of smooth golden sand, with just an occasional interruption, from the Costa del Maresme to the Mar Menor.

Water Sports

With literally millions of holidaymakers heading for the different coastal resorts every year, provisions are made for all the various types of water sports. Among the most popular are windsurfing, waterskiing and scuba diving, along with underwater fishing. Courses are available in most of the large centres which have trained instructors and the necessary equipment for hire. There are also opportunities for canoeing on the Costa Cálida and the Costa del Azahar where information and advice can be obtained from the CIAS Underwater Research and Activities Centre on the Calle José M Haros 18a, Valencia (☎ 335 60 81).

Yachting and Boating
There are so many ports and pleasure harbours all along the eastern costas that any novice who is interested in sailing will find ample opportunities to learn. At the same time, experienced sailors can charter a boat to suit their own requirements. Visiting yachtsmen are also well catered for in the various recreational ports which may well provide a restaurant, bar and swimming pool in addition to a club house, a chandlery and all the usual services. Some of the busy fishing ports have hardly any space available for visitors although even the most crowded will offer assistance in an emergency. Much the same applies to many of the tiny harbours which are frequently inaccessible under adverse conditions and give little or no protection in bad weather. Submerged rocks and shifting sandbanks are another problem so great care should be taken when sailing close inshore or approaching an attractive cove or anchorage. Small boats can be beached in dozens of different places where there may be a few buildings and even basic services.

Telephones

Direct calls can be made from all the provincial capitals, large towns and tourist resorts. For international calls dial 07 and wait for the higher tone. Then, for the United Kingdom, dial 44 followed by the STD number, but remember to drop the 0 at the beginning. For the USA and Canada the identification number is 1 instead of 44. Some resorts have blue 'Telephonica' kiosks which can be used for making international calls. You pay after you have made your call and major credit cards are accepted. It can often be more convenient to phone from a bar than a kiosk. Incidentally, it is also possible to use the toilets in bars without buying a drink.

Tipping

A service charge is often added to a bill whereas the equivalent of VAT is automatically included. However, it is customary to leave a tip unless the food or the service has been unsatisfactory. It is not necessary to tip in bars for drinks provided at the counter but anyone giving a personal service such as guides, usherettes, porters and cloakroom attendants expect a tip. This is also true of taxi drivers and the amount depends entirely on the fare.

Tourist Offices

Many large towns and holiday resorts on the costas have both Tourist Information Offices and Centres of Touristic Initiative. Where neither is available it is usually possible to get advice from the town hall during working hours. Please refer to the lists of Tourist Offices at the end of each chapter's Additional Information section.

Translations of widely-used words

Autopista - Motorway
Calle - Street
Castillo - Castle
Costa - Coast/shore
Iglesia - Church
Mirador - Viewpoint
Museo - Museum
Playa - Beach
Río - River

Travel

Travelling to and from the costas and moving around after arrival are both very simple, with plenty of alternatives to choose from in either case. However, it is worth remembering that the Spanish railways are not compatible with their counterparts across the border in France, so anyone travelling by train is obliged to change at the frontier.

Air

The majority of people arrive in Spain by air these days, either on scheduled services or charter flights. The airport at Girona is convenient for anyone heading for the Costa Brava, whereas Barcelona handles direct flights from the United States and Canada as well as the United Kingdom and most other European countries. Visitors to the Costa Daurada can choose between Barcelona and Reus, near Tarragona, but anyone heading for the Costa Azahar would be more likely to land at Manises, 8km (5 miles) from Valencia. Alicante is the gateway to the Costa Blanca but so far there are no scheduled services to San Javier, near the Mar Menor on the Costa Cálida, although it does cater for charter flights and is in daily contact with Madrid. Internal services operate between most of the main airports in Spain and several smaller ones. Up-to-date information is available from the various airlines and from most travel agencies.

Coaches, Buses and Taxis

All the major cities and several of the larger centres on Spain's eastern costas have their own coach and bus stations. Long distance services mostly operate from Alicante, Barcelona, Murcia and Valencia to other regions throughout the country, while the provincial buses make regular trips to local towns and villages as well as popular holiday resorts. The Tourist Office is the best place to enquire about the various routes and obtain details of current timetables, fares and any concessions that may be available. The buses are generally clean, reliable and a good way of seeing the country. On local services you pay the bus driver but for longer journeys you have to buy a ticket from the bus company's office. Buses are not much cheaper than the railways. However, these can sometimes take rather longer to reach their destinations.

There are plenty of taxis and they are not too expensive. They all have meters and can charge extra for luggage, unsocial hours, waiting time and trips beyond the city limits. Meters are not generally used for longer journeys so it is essential to agree an overall price in advance. Taxis can be hailed in the streets in most large centres and coastal resorts, in addition to which there are plenty of cab ranks as well as radio taxis and usually a one-man firm operating in the more important villages.

Cars, Motor Cycles and Bicycles

Car hire firms operate in the main centres where it is also possible to hire a motor cycle, a moped or a bicycle. You will usually find that about 12 per cent VAT is added to the hire rates.

The International Highway Code applies in Spain exactly as it does in other European countries. Some of the roadsigns you are most likely to see are as follows:

CEDA EL PASO	Give Way
DESPACIO	Slow
DESVIO	Diversion
PASO PROHIBIDO	No entry
CURVA PELIGROSA	Dangerous bend
DIRECCION UNICA	One way street
PROHIBIDO APARCAR	No Parking
OBRAS	Road Works
PELIGRO	Danger
LLEVAR LA DERECHA	Drive on the right
LLEVAR LA IZQUIERDA	Drive on the left

There are motorways from the French frontier down to the Costa Blanca and from south of Barcelona across country through Zaragoza to the Bay of Biscay. They are fast and generally in excellent condition but are mainly subject to tolls which makes them expensive for long journeys. The major roads and highways are almost as good and far more plentiful but they can be crowded, particularly during the holiday season and on the approaches to towns and cities.

Driving Regulations

There are no age restrictions for cyclists although they are also bound by the appropriate rules. No-one under 16 is allowed to drive at all and 18 is the minimum age for taking any vehicle over 75cc out on the roads. Crash helmets are obligatory and motorists must wear seat belts and be adequately insured. British drivers will need an official translation of their UK driving licence if they intend to use it. However, it is actually easier to obtain an International Driving Permit.

Anyone who is used to driving on the left hand side of the road should be particularly careful at roundabouts where the system is the complete opposite of the British one — traffic entering the roundabout has right of way. Also bear in mind that traffic from the right automatically has right of way unless the major route has official priority. Children under 10 should always travel on the back seat and hitchhiking is frowned on but not forbidden. Motorists who intend to use their own cars in Spain should always consult one of the motoring organisations before leaving home because there are other rules and regulations which must be observed. These include documents and various accessories such as a spare set of light bulbs, a red triangle and a first aid kit.

Accidents

If you have an accident telephone 091 for the police or 080 for the fire service if you are in Barcelona. In other towns you should call the operator. The Central Traffic Department runs an assistance service which operates 24 hours a day on every main road in Spain. There is an emergency telephone network on these roads — if you need help you should ask for *auxillio en carretera* (road assistance).

Bail Bonds

An accident in Spain can result in the impounding of your car and, in extreme cases, your being detained pending bail. A Bail Bond can often prevent this and you should obtain one of these from your insurer, together with a Green Card.

Breakdowns

A 24 hour breakdown service is run by the Spanish Motoring Club, called the Real Automovil Club de España (RACE). If you need help call the National Breakdown Centre in Madrid (☎ 91 441 2222) which has an English-speaking service.

Fuel

Fuel is quite widely available although the choice may be restricted in some country areas so it is as well not to go exploring without a reasonably full tank. Very few garages will accept credit cards, especially in the smaller towns. Unleaded petrol (*sin plomo*) is becoming more widely available in the area, particularly in the main centres.

Maps

Among the best are the Michelin maps, the Spanish Mapa de Communicaciones and the extremely detailed versions produced by Almax Editores. Most Tourist Offices will provide useful comprehensive maps of their own areas, especially in places like Barcelona and Valencia.

Parking

Parking is an ever-present problem, especially in small coastal resorts which have only recently started developing their tourist potential. Most of the large towns have both designated parking areas and meters. If you park between blue lines in a car park they indicate that there is a pay and display system.

Speed Limits

In built up areas all vehicles are limited to 60kph (37mph) except where signs indicate a lower limit. Outside built up areas cars are limited to 120kph (74mph) on motorways and 90kph (56mph) on ordinary roads. The limit is 100kph (62mph) on roads with more than one lane in each direction. Vehicles towing a caravan or trailer are limited to 80kph (49mph) on motorways and 70kph (43mph) on other roads.

Rail

The most confusing thing about Spanish trains is that there are so many different types available, from the luxury TEE, or Trans-Europe Express, down to the *semidirecto* that stops at even the smallest hamlets. Wherever possible, the best ones to use are the Talgo variety or the TER trains which are their nearest rivals. Every provincial capital has a railway station with fairly frequent services to centres like Madrid and Barcelona, as well as other parts of the country, with connections on almost every occasion when lines cross. Every city has a RENFE office which is the best place to obtain information, enquire about concessions and buy tickets, which should be obtained in advance wherever possible to avoid confusion, especially for anyone who does not speak the language fluently. Information offices can help you choose whether to opt for a train or catch a bus but they will not issue tickets or make reservations.

Useful Addresses

The Spanish National Tourist Office
57-58 St James's Street
London SW1A 1LD
☎ 44 17 499 0901 (☎ 071 499 0901 in Britain)

The Spanish National Tourist Office
665 Fifth Avenue
New York
N.Y. 10022
☎ (1212) 759 88 22

The Spanish National Tourist Office
60 Bloor Street West, 201
Toronto
Ontario M4W 3B8

The United Kingdom Consulate
Av. Diagonal 477 (08036)
Barcelona
☎ 322 21 51

The United States Consulate
Via Laietana 33 (08003)
Barcelona
☎ 319 95 50

The Canadian Consulate
Via Augusta 125 (08006)
Barcelona
☎ 209 06 34

INDEX